ADULTING IN THE WILD

Life Skills To Gain Independence, Transcend Instant Ramen, And Take On The World

KIMBERLY EATON

Contents

For Ryan and Kyra,
my greatest teachers

Introduction

Have you ever found yourself standing in the middle of a grocery store with a shopping cart filled with instant noodles, cereal, and a suspiciously large amount of cheese, wondering how adult life has led you to this moment? Or perhaps you received your first paycheck, only to realize you have no idea whether to splurge on that concert ticket or squirrel it away into some savings account your Uncle Gene keeps mentioning at family dinners. Welcome to the whimsical world of 'adulting' - where the struggle is real, but so are the opportunities to conquer it with panache.

Why is this guide essential for you, the digital-native teen poised to conquer the world? I have noticed a significant gap in our school curriculums—a lack of emphasis on vital life skills. Today's 'adulting' is not your parents 'adulting'. The rules have changed, and this book equips you with the most current, up-to-date strategies for excelling in life.

'Adulting' - a term that might make some roll their eyes so hard they see their brain. I've been there—staring down at my first tax forms like they were written in an alien language...using hair conditioner to shave my legs because it was cheaper than shaving cream...trying to make one paper product (toilet paper) substitute for the other three paper products (tissue, napkins, paper towels) that I couldn't afford...and I was consuming more boxed mac and cheese than I thought humanly possible.

I learned the hard way, but you don't have to. My mission is to pass on these critical life skills that I gathered from various experts and mentors and a few embarrassing mistakes. Though much about adulting has changed, instant noodles never die.

I know you have the potential to master this adulting thing. With each chapter, you'll find yourself better equipped to handle tasks like managing your finances, making decisions about your education and career, understanding the gig economy, maintaining your mental health, and navigating relationships. And in a world where your online presence can be as influential as your real-life one, we'll address modern challenges like managing your social media footprint and navigating the complex world of cybersecurity.

This book is your down-to-earth, practical toolkit designed to bridge the Grand Canyon-sized gap between the end of formal education and the start of real-world adult life.

By the time you turn the final page, you won't just be more informed; you'll be equipped, confident, and inspired to take on the world of adulthood. You'll understand not just how to do things but why they matter.

So, dear reader, as we embark on this journey together, remember: adulting might feel like assembling IKEA furniture without the instructions, but with this book in hand, you're about to become a master builder. Let's do this!

ONE

Gimme Shelter

> *"Fries or salad?" sums up every adult decision you must make.*
>
> Aparna Nancherla

Have you got your own place yet? Probably not, unless you've hit an income jackpot. These days, half of young adults in America are still living with their folks. And that's completely fine. If you have that safe spot to crash, be thankful. The road to independence is not a straight shot anymore. Sure, you might dream of living solo, surviving on pizza scraps, and partying into the early hours—but hang in there; your time will come. Life's tough, so if you have food, a roof over your head, and someone who cares about keeping you safe, consider yourself fortunate.

Or have you already flown the nest? Bunking on a lumpy futon in someone's converted garage? Stuffing t-shirts into your new dorm's tiny drawers? Sitting on the floor of your empty new apartment? Here is the basic domestic info you need to keep those instant noodles coming.

I Didn't Burn It This Time

So, you've just graduated from the madhouse known as high school, and you're about to dive into the "real world"—a place where meals don't just appear by magic. What's the first challenge? Nope, it's not the mountain of laundry (though that's a close second); it's figuring out how to feed yourself. Wave goodbye to those home-cooked meals and the always full carton of milk. Say hello to Taco Tuesday—where the tacos don't make themselves.

Learning to cook isn't just about avoiding a diet of cereal for every meal; it's about making sure you don't turn your kitchen into a hazard zone and occasionally impressing your friends on Instagram with something that looks edible. But before you freak out about using knives and playing with fire, let's dial it back to **the basics**. You can whip up a decent meal without going broke, setting your kitchen on fire, or completely losing your mind.

Starting to cook can feel as daunting as choosing a Netflix show from thousands of options. **Keep it simple.** Start with foolproof recipes like one-pot pasta, vibrant stir-fries, or the ever-popular tacos. These aren't just meals; they're your training wheels in the kitchen. Who knows, you might feel like a pro or at least not a danger to yourself and others by next Taco Tuesday.

If you don't already have some favorite recipes, check out these **recipe apps** with free subscription options like **Yummly, AllRecipes, and BigOven.** Of course, YouTube videos can show you how to boil pasta, scramble an egg, and grill your veggies. Practice a few easy dishes that appeal to you, and when you do cook, make a big batch that you can use for lunches or dinners during the week. **Leftovers** can be saved in freezer bags but should be consumed within the month. To be safe, though, label your leftovers with dates and contents. Nothing derails your newfound adulting skills like food poisoning from mystery meat from the Ice Age.

Here is some **kitchen equipment** you can't do without if you're building your new kitchen from scratch:

- Plates, glasses and silverware
- Plastic storage containers of different sizes
- Chef's knife
- Measuring cups and spoons
- Two sizes of cutting boards
- Mixing bowls
- Strainers for pasta and veggies
- Baking sheets and pizza sheet
- Glass baking dish
- Can opener
- Whisk
- Metal tongs
- Metal spatula

This Looks Edible

Let's break down the food hype and get back to basics with **macronutrients**, the big bosses of your dietary intake: carbohydrates, proteins, and fats. **Carbs** are not the enemy—they are your primary energy source, powering everything from your brain functions to your soccer skills. Think of them as the gas that keeps your car running. Whole grains, fruits, and veggies are like premium fuel - the **fiber** to keep your digestive system primed and pumping correctly. On the other hand, too many sugary snacks?

That's like putting soda in your gas tank—sure, it's liquid, but it will wreak havoc.

Proteins are your body's building blocks, vital for muscle repair and growth—essential whether you're a gym enthusiast or just trying to haul your backpack around. Foods like chicken, tofu, and legumes are your go-to allies here. And don't forget **fats—the good ones**, like avocados, nuts, natural peanut butter, and olive oil, keep your cells happy and your brain sharp. They're like the oil that keeps everything running smoothly without any squeaks.

How do you balance all three? Picture your plate as a pie chart: half filled with fruits and vegetables, one quarter with proteins, and the other quarter with whole grains or other carb sources. Add a small dash of healthy fats, and voila! You have a meal that would make both your taste buds and cells do a happy dance. Splurge on a real pie occasionally.

Moving on from solid to liquid, let's talk about hydration. **Water** isn't just something you dive into during summer pool parties—it's essential for your body's daily functions. From keeping your temperature in check to flushing out toxins and aiding digestion, water is the MVP of your bodily functions. But how much do you need? While the adage suggests eight glasses daily, your mileage may vary depending on your activity level, climate, and diet.

Here's a pro tip: do not wait until you're parched. Carry a **reusable water bottle** and take sips throughout the day. Not a fan of plain water? Jazz it up with slices of lemon, cucumber, or a splash of juice. Herbal teas count too, and they can be a cozy alternative during those chilly months. Just remember that **caffeinated** drinks can *dehydrate* you—yes, that includes your beloved energy drinks and even that innocent-looking iced tea.

Now, let's decode the mystic runes known as **nutrition labels**. These labels are your cheat sheets for making informed food choices. Have you ever picked up a packet of nuts and seen something like "calories, 160; total fat, 14g"? That is not random data. Those numbers tell you how much energy you're getting and from what sources. Here's the kicker: pay attention to **serving size**. It's easy to binge-eat those chips, thinking the whole bag is one serving, but often, it's not. And suddenly, your snack has turned into a full-blown meal.

Look beyond calories. Check out the fiber content (your tummy will thank you), **sugars** (less is more), and proteins (your body's buddy). And **sodium**—watch out for it. Too much can lead to high blood pressure. Treat these labels like a map that guides you through the nutritional landscape, helping you to make choices that align with your health goals. Unfortunately, ketchup is not a vegetable.

Finally, let's talk about meal prep. It's a fantastic way to take control of your diet, save time, and dodge those unhealthy impulse eats. Start simple: **plan your meals** for the week on a Sunday. This does not mean cooking all day; get a basic idea of what you'll eat. Batch cook some staples like rice and proteins or chop veggies. Store them in the fridge, and you have a weekly mix-and-match buffet.

You've got Taco Tuesday down, so why not try Meatless Monday or Stir-Fry Friday? This not only adds variety but also simplifies shopping and prep. Remember, the goal isn't to chain you to the kitchen but to free you from the daily "what's for dinner?" panic. With these tricks up your sleeve, you'll be whipping up quick, healthy meals faster than you can say, "Order pizza!"

Heading to the market? Never enter a grocery store without a list. A **grocery list** is your battle plan, your strategy to avoid the siren call of unnecessary snacks and impulse buys. Start by **planning your meals for the week**—all of them, including **snacks.** This might sound like overkill, but it saves you time, money, and extra calories. Categorize your list by store sections (produce, dairy, meats, snacks) to avoid backtracking and the temptation lurking in every aisle. Learn the layout of your favorite market! Remember, the grocery store is a maze designed to keep you inside as long as possible. But if you stick to your list, you're in and out like a ninja.

Never enter a grocery store when you are **hungry.** When faced with every kind of food imaginable on an empty stomach, your next meal will be Doritos and four bags of half-priced Halloween candy you just saw in the checkout line. Don't do it, friends. Have a sandwich before you head to the market.

It All Comes Out in the Wash

Imagine this: it's **laundry day,** and your favorite white shirt emerges from the washer looking like a tie-dye project gone wrong, all because it partied too hard with a rogue red sock. Welcome to the perilous world of laundry, where colors bleed and that one sweater could suddenly fit your cat. But fear not, soapy soldier. Arm yourself with these laundry tips, and you'll conquer the chaos with finesse.

Sorting is not just for wizards and their hats. In the laundry realm, **sorting** is your first line of defense against the tragedy of **color transfer.** You're not just separating the darks from the lights (though that's a great start); you need to consider **fabric types** and how lonely your delicates feel when mixed with the rough crowd of jeans and towels. Sort by color, fabric type, and soil level if you have very **dirty duds.** Hot tip: always wash new colored clothes **separately** the first time—their true colors can turn on you faster than a plot twist in a teen drama.

Those **cryptic symbols** on your clothing tags are not just there for decoration—they are the secret to keeping your clothes in top-notch condition. Think of them as the care instructions you never got for that "adulting" thing. Each wavy symbol tells you how to wash, dry, iron, and avoid turning your new cashmere sweater into a doll-sized catastrophe. For instance, a tub with wavy lines means machine wash, while a tub with a hand means hand wash only. If there's a cross over the tumble dry icon, you'd better air dry unless you want to shrink into your clothes. Hang it to dry in your shower.

Stains are like the uninvited party crashers of the fabric world. But instead of turning away in defeat, greet them with your stain-removal arsenal. Here is your basic combat kit: **Stain spray** is a given. **What also works is white vinegar, baking soda, and the classic** hydrogen peroxide. Wine spill? Salt and cold water can save your dignity. Grease stain from that pizza you swore was a salad? Dish soap is your new best friend. Remember, the golden rule of stain removal is to **treat it quickly**; a stain delayed is a stain forever stayed. Blot, don't rub; you might salvage that shirt from becoming another cleaning rag.

You've washed, dried, and conquered stains. Now comes the art of **folding**. Resist the urge to shove everything in your drawer like you're stuffing a turkey. Proper folding not only **saves space** but also **prevents wrinkles** and preserves the life of your clothes. T-shirts can be folded military style for maximum drawer efficiency; pants are best folded along the seams. And socks? They like to cuddle, so fold them together. As for organizing, **keep it intuitive**. Store frequently used items at prime real estate locations (top drawers or eye-level shelves) and the rarely used (like that ugly holiday sweater) in the back or up high. Your future self will thank you every morning as you effortlessly pick out today's outfit without turning your closet into a war zone.

Where are My Keys? Keeping a Clean Room

Let's face it: the state of your room can either be a haven of peace or a chaotic realm where even the bravest souls fear to tread. Maintaining a clean room isn't just about appeasing your parents; it's about crafting a space to chill, study, and maybe even find that other sock. This is not about turning you into Cinderella—no singing birds required—but about establishing a practical, **doable system** that keeps your personal space less a disaster zone and more like a Zen garden where you can relax.

Understanding the difference between what needs **daily attention** and what can be tackled weekly is your first step to not feeling overwhelmed. Daily tasks are all about maintenance. This means **making your bed**, dealing with dirty clothes (not the sniff test— actual decisions), and keeping surfaces clear. Why make your bed? Because it visually sets your space to 'ready.' It signals to your brain that the chaos of sleep is over and the order of the day is beginning. It is surprisingly satisfying to leave your home with your bed looking straight out of a catalog, even if it will be a mess again tonight.

Weekly tasks can be more in-depth. This is when you vacuum or sweep, change your sheets (yes, they need changing), and do a more thorough dusting. Think of your weekly clean as a reset button that keeps your room from sliding back into the primal chaos from which it barely emerged. Splitting tasks this way ensures you're not spending hours daily; you're maintaining through the week and diving deeper when you have more time.

Let's get down to brass tacks. **Daily cleaning isn't deep cleaning**; it's about not letting the mess pile up. Start with the bed. Next, tackle any clothes that have tried to escape. Dirty ones go in the hamper; clean ones get folded or hung up. Deal with the dishes; a stray cup or plate should head straight to the kitchen. If waking up to roaches eating last night's mozzarella sticks does not entice you, **never leave food uncovered** on the counter overnight. Lastly, a quick wipe-down of your most-used surfaces, like your desk or nightstand, can keep dust and clutter at bay. Keeping these tasks short and sweet means you are more likely to stick to them.

There's actual psychology behind why a clean room feels good. **Clutter** can significantly increase **stress and anxiety**. It overloads your senses like multitasking, making you feel frazzled and forget-ful. I'm bugging you about the bed because making your bed every morning is a small ritual that can set the tone for the day. You're taking control of your environment and, by extension, a bit of your mental state. Plus, there is nothing quite like the promise of slipping into a well-made bed after a long day. It's a daily gift to yourself.

Now, decluttering isn't just about throwing things away; it's about creating a space that feels good. Start by categorizing your stuff. **Keep, donate, or trash**. Be honest about what you use and what's just taking up space. Once you've pared down, organize what's left. Every item should have a home, whether a drawer, a shelf, or a bin. Use organizers or boxes to keep similar items together. This helps you find things more efficiently and stops items from wandering off. The less you own, the less you have to clean—simplicity is king.

Time management can be the hero or the villain in your cleaning saga. Set specific times for your daily and weekly cleaning tasks, and treat them like any other non-negotiable appointment. Maybe you make your bed right before brushing your teeth or handle laundry every Sunday afternoon. By **scheduling** these tasks, you remove the guesswork and reduce the chance of them being overlooked. Remember, consistency is critical; the more regular your cleaning schedule, the less time each task takes.

The Rent is Due Already?

Alright, so you're moving into your first place. Exciting, right? But with great apartments come significant responsibilities, like understanding the jungle of paperwork known as your **lease agreement.** This document is the rulebook for your stay—it outlines what you can and cannot do, how much you'll pay, and what happens if you turn the living room into a circus tent. First things first: **read it thoroughly.** Yes, it's about as exciting as watching paint dry, but it's crucial. You need to know your obligations, like how much notice you need to give before moving out and what your landlord will take care of (hopefully everything broken). Also, get familiar with terms like 'subletting' and 'security deposit'—they will be more beneficial than your high school trigonometry.

Now, let's talk about **co-signers.** If you are fresh out of high school or college, there's a good chance your landlord will want a co-signer. This is someone like a parent or guardian who agrees to pay your rent if you decide to spend all your money on concert tickets instead. It's like having a safety net, but one that will remind you at every family gathering about the time they had to cover your rent.

Moving on to **roommates.** Living with someone is great until you discover they're a serial dishes-leaver. Set some **ground rules** early on to avoid turning your home into a battleground over whose turn it is to take out the trash. Discuss everything from who cleans what and when to how late is too late for playing death metal on a weekday. It's about respect, sharing responsibilities, and not leaving passive-aggressive notes on the fridge. Be transparent about **finances,** too—decide how to split the rent, utilities, and grocery bills. And if you're thinking of **getting a pet**, make sure everyone is on board (and the lease allows it) unless you want to find out the hard way that your roommate is allergic to cats.

Budgeting is your best friend when it comes to renting. Before you sign that lease, do the math. Can you afford this place once you factor in utilities, food, internet, and your coffee habit? Living within your means is essential, even if that means passing on the loft with the rooftop pool. Late rent payments can lead to fees or a very unhappy landlord knocking at your door. Always aim to **pay your rent on time**, or early if possible, to keep that landlord-tenant relationship smoother than your morning smoothie.

Communication is the glue that holds the delicate balance of tenant life together. Tell your landlord immediately if there is a problem with the apartment, like a leaky faucet or mysterious noises in the wall. They are there to help (and it is their job), and dealing with issues early can prevent them from becoming more significant, costlier problems. Keeping open lines of communication with your roommates is equally crucial. Don't let minor annoyances build up until you're all starring in your own reality show drama. **Talk things out** like the mature adults you are rapidly becoming.

Finally, what do you do when you're **ready to move out**? It sounds far away now but will come faster than you think. Leave the place better than you found it—**clean thoroughly**, make any necessary repairs, and take photos once everything is spotless. Why? Because you want that **security deposit** back. That's right, the money you forgot about after you paid it a year ago. It's free money—if you leave your apartment in good shape. Remember to give your landlord a **forwarding address** for that last utility bill or your security deposit refund if you're lucky. And just like that, you're out, hopefully onto bigger and better adventures, with some extra rental savvy in your back pocket.

I Can Fix It: A Teen's Toolkit

Have you ever faced a dripping faucet at 2 AM or a door that won't close properly? Before you call your local handyman or—worse—your overeager uncle with zero DIY skills but maximum enthusiasm, let's arm you with the basics. Knowing **a few handy skills** can save you money (your future self chilling on a self-bought yacht will thank you) and give you the independence and confidence to say, "I've got this!" Because adulthood is just one long episode of "Fixer Upper"—minus the charming hosts.

Building your toolkit is like assembling a superhero squad—each member has a unique role crucial for victory. **Start with the basics:** a reliable hammer, a couple of screwdrivers (both flathead and Phillips), a tape measure (because guessing measurements is the DIY version of playing Russian roulette), an adjustable wrench, a set of Allen keys (those L shaped bars), and, of course, duct tape (the solution to 73% of life's problems, in rainbow colors!). These tools can handle most minor repairs and projects around the house (I'm looking at YOU, evil and unworkable IKEA bed frame instructions!) A level is also handy to keep things from looking like a funhouse project. Store these tools in a sturdy toolbox or a drawer that is easy to access—there's nothing worse than hunting for a screwdriver when you're in the DIY zone.

Let's tackle the common culprits: **leaky faucets and holes in the wall.** First, the faucet. This can usually be fixed by replacing a washer or tightening a few nuts. Shut off the water supply (because the only thing worse than a leaky faucet is an indoor fountain), remove the faucet, and replace any worn-out washers with new ones from the hardware store. As for that hole in the wall—no, not the one with philosophical implications—the actual hole, is nothing a bit of spackle can't fix. Apply it over the hole, smooth it out, and once it dries, sand it down to match the rest of the wall. A dab of paint later, and it's like your little sister never practiced her ninja stars indoors. **Questions?** Google it, try YouTube, or chase down the Home Depot associate wandering aimlessly around the store.

Wielding your toolkit like Thor's hammer might make you feel invincible, but here's where we pump the brakes. Safety is crucial. Always wear protective gear like **safety goggles** and **gloves** when doing anything that could send debris flying or involves chemicals. Know your limits—**electricity and complex plumbing are NOT DIY-friendly zones**. Tinkering with wires is not the same as fixing a lamp. One wrong move, and you might reenact that scene from your favorite horror movie. **Do not mess with this**. When in doubt, call a professional. It's cool to be the hero, but it's cooler to have all your fingers and eyebrows intact.

Feel the DIY bug biting? Great! It's time to **upgrade those skills**. The internet is a treasure trove of resources. Websites like Instructables, DIY Network, and YouTube channels dedicated to home repairs can be invaluable. They offer **step-by-step tutorials**, from fixing a leaky roof to creating your own bookshelf. Consider a basic home improvement course at a local community college or workshop for more structured learning. Remember, the goal isn't just fixing things around the house but building skills that'll last a lifetime—like learning to cook but with more power tools and less chance of accidentally making a salad.

TWO

Pennies From Heaven

I magine this: you've just stumbled upon a magical piggy bank that refills every time you spend money. Sounds pretty sweet, right? Unfortunately, in the real world, money doesn't grow on trees or magically appear in piggy banks. It comes from that thing you might not be too fond of yet—work. Managing your money isn't just about counting cash; it's about making sure you're not at zero by the end of the month. So, let's dive into the mystical **world of finances**, where understanding the difference between fixed and variable income is more exciting than your latest TikTok scroll.

Money for Nothing

First off, let's decode the riddle of fixed versus variable income. **Fixed income** is like that reliable friend who shows up every day at the same time with the exact number of chips you need for your snack. If you're interning, this is your regular paycheck from a part-time job or a stipend. It's predictable, which is great for planning your monthly splurges and necessities.

Then there's **variable income**, the wild card friend who surprises you with concert tickets on a Tuesday or suddenly needs a couch to crash on. This could be money you make from freelancing, babysitting, or that Etsy shop where you sell your knitted hats. It's less predictable, but it spices up your financial life with extra cash flows at unexpected times.

Now, onto **balancing a checkbook**. Wait, don't roll your eyes yet! Knowing how to manage a checkbook—or its digital equivalent— is crucial. It's tracking what comes in and what goes out. Simply put, make sure the money leaving your account isn't playing a vanishing act without your permission. Regularly check your bank statements against your own records. Mistakes happen—like when you were charged thrice for that single burrito—so stay sharp.

Creating a **budget** isn't just for adults with nine-to-five jobs. As a teen, it's the blueprint for your financial house. Start by listing your total income and then subtract your expenses—start with the necessities like phone bills or that streaming subscription (because who can live without their favorite shows?). What you have left can be directed towards savings or splurging on things like games, clothes, or whatever floats your boat. Remember, a good budget is flexible. It grows and shrinks with your financial situation, so adjust it as your income changes.

Gone are the days of **tracking expenses** in dusty old ledgers. Numerous **apps** can now manage your finances with a swipe and a tap. Use these digital tools to watch where your money is going closely—kind of like how you track who's winning in your fantasy football league. Seeing the numbers can be a real eye-opener and might just make you rethink buying that fourth pair of sneakers.

Setting **financial goals** is like deciding whether you want to save up for that epic summer road trip or to afford a car for said trip. Short-term goals can be as simple as saving for a new game or concert tickets. Long-term goals require more patience, including saving for college or a car. Both are important and balancing them is key. Keep your eyes on the prize(s), and adjust your saving habits accordingly to hit those targets.

Your financial situation will change; that's just a part of life. Maybe you get a raise at your job or decide to quit to focus on school. Your budget should be a living document that evolves as you do. **Flexibility** in your financial planning ensures you can always make the most of your money, rain or shine.

Finally, let's tackle a real-world skill—**calculating a tip**. Whether you're dining out, getting a haircut, or using any service where tipping is customary, knowing how to calculate a tip is essential. A simple way to calculate a 15-20% tip without a calculator is to double the amount of the tax. So, if your meal costs $20, a $4 tip (**20% of your bill**) is a generous way to show appreciation for good service.

Keep track of your income, manage your expenses, and always remember—every penny counts, especially when it's heading toward something that matters to you. Let those pennies rain from heaven, and catch them with a well-prepared bucket.

Take Some Credit

Let's talk **credit**, and no, not the kind you get for acing a pop quiz. We're diving into the realm of credit scores and credit cards, a territory that might sound about as complicated as your last break-up. But fear not, my young friend, because understanding credit is a game-changer for your financial health, and it doesn't require a PhD in economics, just a bit of savvy.

Your **credit score** is like a report card for your financial habits. It tells potential lenders how good you are at paying back money you borrow. This number ranges from 300 to 850; higher is better here. It's calculated based on a few things: your payment history (do you pay your bills on time?), the amounts you owe (maxing out cards is a no-go), the length of your credit history, new credit, and the types of credit you use. Managing these factors well boosts your credit score, which can affect everything from **renting an apartment** to getting a phone plan. It can even **influence job opportunities** in fields like finance, where they equate financial responsibility with job performance.

Now, let's break down the credit cards—secured versus unsecured. A **secured credit card** is like training wheels for credit. You put down a deposit (usually a few hundred dollars), which is now your credit limit. If you pay your credit card on time and prove your worthiness to the credit gods, they will slowly increase your spending funds. It's a way to build or rebuild credit, making it a stellar choice for first-timers. Then there's the **unsecured credit card**, which doesn't require a cash deposit and often comes with reward points or cash back perks. Sounds great, right? It can be if you handle it wisely.

Using a credit card **responsibly** is an art form. It's tempting to treat it as free money, but remember, every swipe is a loan you'll need to repay every single month. To stay safe, try to **pay off your balance in full** each month to avoid interest charges, which can pile up quicker than likes on a viral video. If you can't pay in full, aim to **keep your balance below 30% of your credit limit**. This helps your credit score and keeps your debt from ballooning. And be cautious with cash advances; they often come with high fees and interest rates that kick in immediately.

Loans are like relationships—good ones can enrich your life, but bad ones can leave you stressed and paying for past mistakes. There are several types, including student loans for education, auto loans for that sweet ride, and personal loans, which can cover just about anything from medical bills to vacations. Each type affects your financial future differently. **Student loans**, for example, are considered 'good debt' because an education can increase earning potential. However, it would be best if you absolutely considered the total cost over time, including interest. **Auto loans** depreciate because cars lose value, so paying them off quickly is wise. **Personal loans** require careful consideration to ensure the long-term benefits outweigh the costs.

Managing debt is crucial, especially if juggling multiple loans or credit cards. It's all about strategy. First, understand the terms of your debts: **interest rates, due dates, and minimum payments**. From there, consider tactics like **the debt avalanche**, where you pay off debts from highest to lowest interest rate. This method saves money on interest over time, freeing up more cash as each debt is paid off. Another approach is **the debt snowball** method, where you pay off the smallest debts first, gaining momentum and motivation as each one is cleared. Whichever strategy you choose, the key is consistency and a clear focus on your end goal: **becoming debt-free** and aiming toward your financial goals. Fun stuff, right?

Wheeling and Dealing

You have a lot to offer! Understanding **what your skills are worth** in the marketplace is not just about feeding your ego; it's about ensuring you're not shortchanged for your hard work. Before you even step into a negotiation, doing your homework is crucial. What are people in your position, with your experience level, making in your area? You need to **arm yourself** with this information. Websites like Glassdoor, PayScale, and LinkedIn Salary can be your best friends here, offering insights into **what others in your field earn**. Think of it as knowing the rules of the game before you start playing. This research helps you understand what you should earn and gives you the confidence to ask for it.

Now, let's shift gears to the **art of negotiation**. It might sound like something only high-powered executives need to know, but trust me, this is a skill as essential as being able to find the best memes in under thirty seconds. When **discussing salary**, it's important to keep the conversation **professional and focused**. Begin by expressing enthusiasm for the role, then transition to your compensation expectations. It's like starting a road trip with a killer playlist; it sets the tone for a smooth ride. Use the **salary data** you've gathered as a baseline, and be prepared to explain why you deserve this amount. Maybe your stellar grades, unique skills, or internships have prepared you uniquely for this role. Whatever it is, make it clear that you're not pulling numbers out of thin air—they're **based on solid data and your qualifications.**

However, while confidence is key, arrogance is the locked door no one wants to open. This brings us to **common negotiation pitfalls**. One major mistake is accepting the first offer too quickly. It's like grabbing the first slice of pizza out of the box; it might satisfy you in the short term, but you might regret not waiting for the pepperoni one coming up next. Take your time to consider the offer. Don't be afraid to politely counter the offer if it's below your expectations. Another blunder is not being prepared to walk away. Sometimes, the best deal you negotiate is the one you do not take. If the terms don't meet your needs or undervalue your skills, **be prepared to decline**. It's better to hold out for a position that recognizes your worth.

Choosing when to accept or decline a job offer can feel like trying to decide on a movie at 1 AM—you're tired, you want to make a decision, but you also want to make sure it's the right one. **When an offer is on the table**, weigh it against your predetermined criteria: salary, benefits, work culture, and growth opportunities. It's not just about the money—consider whether this position will help you advance your career or if it aligns with your long-term goals. If an offer **checks most of your boxes**, and the salary is within your acceptable range, then go for it. However, if the cons outweigh the pros, it might be time to say, "Thanks, but no thanks," and keep looking. Remember, every job offer is not just a potential paycheck; it's a stepping stone in your career path, so choose the stones that lead you in the direction you want to go.

Jumping Overboard

Let's talk about the **financial deep end**, where the waters of money management can get pretty choppy. Here's where even the savviest swimmers might struggle—dealing with debt traps, the siren call of impulse buying, dodgy financial scams, and the black hole of tech overspending. Navigating these treacherous currents requires more than just a good boat. You need a solid game plan.

Imagine this: you're short on cash, and suddenly, an ad pops up promising instant money with a payday loan. It's tempting, right? Here's the catch—these loans often come with astronomically high interest rates that can turn a small loan into a **mountain of debt** faster than you can say "bankruptcy." It's like being given a small water wing to swim across the ocean. Not so helpful, right? And then there's credit card debt. It starts innocently enough—a purchase here, a bill there. But without careful management, it's like a snowball rolling downhill, growing bigger and gathering speed. The key here is **vigilance**. Keep an eye on your spending, and always, always **pay more than the minimum** if you can. This helps you dodge the compound interest that can make paying off these debts feel like trying to climb out of a well with butter on your hands.

Now, onto **impulse buying**. It's like walking into a candy store and buying everything that catches your eye, except it's not candy; it's stuff you might not even need. The immediate gratification might feel great, but the aftermath? Not so much. This habit can sabotage your budget faster than a hacker can say "gotcha." So, how do you combat this? **Start by identifying your triggers**. Are you a comfort shopper, a boredom buyer, or a deal-chaser? Recognizing why you make impulsive purchases is the first step to curbing them. Next, **try the 24-hour rule**. If you want something, wait 24 hours. If you still think it's essential, then consider buying it. Often, this cooling-off period helps the initial "gotta have it" frenzy to fade, saving you from buyer's remorse and an unhappy wallet.

In the Internet age, **financial scams** have gone digital, and they are trickier than ever. Scammers love targeting teens because they're often new to managing their money. One common scam? **Phishing emails** that look like they're from a legit company asking you to "verify" your account details. The moment you click on that link and fill in your info, you've just handed your keys to the scammers. **Always verify the source** before clicking on any suspicious links. Look very closely at the sender's email address: often, there are letters or numbers in places that do not look legit. Another popular scam? The **"You've won a prize" scam** asks you to pay a small fee to claim a large prize. Spoiler alert: the prize doesn't exist. If it sounds too good to be true, it probably is. Delete it! Keep your personal information under lock and key, and always double-check before sharing any details online.

Tech gadgets are the ultimate temptation. They're sleek, shiny, and promise to make life so much easier. But here's the thing—tech companies are brilliant at making you feel like you need an upgrade yearly. Ask yourself if your current device meets your needs. Is your 2-year old iPhone still your best buddy? Can it survive another year? If the answer is yes, stick with what you have. If you do need to upgrade, **consider buying refurbished** devices. They're often just as good as the new ones but at a fraction of the cost. Plus, you get to pat yourself on the back for being economically and environmentally savvy.

The Taxman

Ah, taxes—the favorite topic of...well, no one really, unless you're an accountant or someone who gets a kick out of complex math and legal jargon. Let's break down the basics of income taxes without making it feel like a root canal, shall we?

Think of the government as a massive GoFundMe, but instead of funding your art project, it's all about roads, schools, and your local park benches. Your contribution to this cause is called **federal income tax**, based on—surprise—how much money you make. Now, the fun part: **tax brackets**. These aren't the brackets you fill out during March Madness. Instead, they determine the percentage of your income you owe to the government. The more you make, the higher the percentage you pay. However, it's not as straightforward as it sounds because these are marginal rates, meaning they only apply to the income within a specific range. This system ensures that your first dollar is taxed less than the last.

Next up, **deductions and credits** are the power-ups in your tax game. Deductions lower your taxable income. For example, if you earn $30,000 and have $3,000 in deductions, you only get taxed on $27,000. Credits, on the other hand, reduce your tax bill dollar-for-dollar. So, if you owe $1,000 in taxes and have a $200 credit, you only owe $800. Keep these in your financial toolkit; they can save you money.

Landing your first job feels incredible until you get your first paycheck and notice it's not quite the amount you expected. Welcome to the world of **payroll taxes**. When you start a job, you'll fill out a **W-4 form**. This little piece of paper is crucial because it tells your employer how much tax to withhold from your paycheck. Claiming "zero" means more money gets taken out of each paycheck (safer for avoiding owing tax in April), but claiming more allowances means less tax withheld (risky if you claim too many).

Reading a paycheck stub is the next skill to master. It outlines your earnings and what is deducted—think federal and state taxes, Social Security, Medicare, and maybe even contributions to a retirement plan. It might look like alphabet soup initially, but understanding where your money is going is critical to financial awareness. We'll dive into more info on understanding your first paycheck in the next chapter.

If you're a **freelancer or gig worker**, welcome to the world of **self-employment taxes**. Unlike traditional jobs where employers handle your tax withholdings, freelancers are their own bosses and tax managers. This means paying self-employment tax, which covers your Social Security and Medicare contributions. You'll also need to make estimated quarterly tax payments to avoid penalties. Keeping meticulous records of your income and expenses becomes your new hobby because every receipt saved is a potential deduction from your taxable income.

Every January, you will receive a **W-2 form** in the mail. This document itemizes your annual earnings and taxes paid for the prior year. To begin doing your taxes, **Turbo Tax online** is a great way to get started. It handles everything and walks you through each step, including what to do with that W-2 form. You'll know immediately whether a wonderful tax refund is headed your way, or if you owe Uncle Sam more of your hard-earned cash.

Understanding the layers of taxation is like realizing there was a backside to your favorite album's cover art all along. Federal taxes are consistent across the U.S., but **state taxes**? They're as varied as your pizza toppings. Some states, like Florida and Texas, don't have an income tax, while others, like California and New York, will take a more significant bite out of your paycheck. Knowing **the tax landscape of your state** is crucial for budgeting, especially if you're thinking about moving or working across state lines.

Taxes might not be the most thrilling topic, but they're a part of adult life. Getting a handle on them means you're better prepared to make smart financial decisions, from negotiating your salary to planning your budget. Remember, every dollar you save on taxes is another dollar in your pocket for that dream road trip, killer gadget, or even a fancy dinner out.

THREE

Path to the Paycheck

> *College is like looking both ways before crossing the street and then getting hit by an airplane.*
>
> Anonymous

D o you feel like your future career is a giant puzzle and you're holding a piece that doesn't quite fit? Don't sweat it! This chapter is all about transforming that odd puzzle piece into a perfect match for the jigsaw that is the job market. Let's navigate the winding roads of career exploration where your passion meets your paycheck.

That Sounds Cool

Imagine you're the star of a reality TV show where the grand prize is your dream job. But here's the twist: you have to identify what that dream job is. The first step is pinpointing your **interests and skills.** This isn't just about what you're good at—it's also about **what lights a fire** in your belly. Do you love doodling or crafting stories? Maybe a career in graphic design or writing is your calling. Do you geek out on numbers? Fascinated by how gadgets work? Engineering or accounting might just be your arena.

But how do you translate a hobby like gaming or a talent for calming down your drama-queen friend into a career? Here's where a bit of **self-assessment** comes in handy. Tools like the **Meyers-Briggs Personality test** aren't just fun quizzes—they're insightful **resources** that help map out how your traits could thrive in specific careers. They can show you whether you're more suited to front-line leadership roles or brainstorming sessions in a think tank.

Now, let's talk about **passion**. It's the secret sauce that can turn a mundane job into a fulfilling career. Think about it. Would you rather wake up groaning every Monday or jump out of bed excited to get to work? Work doesn't feel like a chore when you choose a career path that aligns with what you genuinely enjoy. Plus, passion can drive you to excel, opening doors to promotions and opportunities. It helps connect the dots between what you love doing and how you can make a living out of it.

Staying updated on **job market trends** is like having a forecast that helps you plan your career wardrobe. Emerging industries like renewable energy, tech, and telemedicine are the new wave of opportunities. Dive into research, attend job fairs, and maybe even set up informational interviews with professionals in fields you're curious about. These are **goldmines** of insights and can sometimes lead directly to job opportunities or internships.

Lastly, let's future-proof your career path. The job market is as stable as a house of cards in a wind tunnel—always changing, always evolving. **Skills in demand** today might be obsolete tomorrow (sorry, typewriter repair experts). Keep an eye on trends, not just in specific job roles but in skills, too. **Adaptability,**

digital literacy, and emotional intelligence are becoming must-haves in almost every field. Consider courses or workshops to polish these competencies, ensuring you remain a valuable player in the job market game.

Why not create a career vision board to lay out the possible landscape of your future job? Grab some magazines, print out images, jot down key skills or inspiring quotes, and create a visual map of your ideal career path. This is a fun, creative way to set your aspirations in stone—or in this case, in paper and glue. Plus, it's a daily visual reminder of where you're headed, keeping you **motivated and focused** as you journey toward your paycheck dreams.

So, as you ponder the pathways to your professional future, remember that aligning your passions with your career is not just a lofty dream—it's a practical strategy for a satisfying and successful work life. Keep exploring, keep learning, and let your interests guide you to a job that doesn't just pay the bills but also brings you joy.

The College Decision

When it comes to life after high school, it's like standing at a massive buffet loaded with tantalizing options. Do you fill your plate with the traditional four-year college experience or go for the quicker, possibly cheaper bite of trade school or community college? Both paths have garnishes and perks, so let's dig in, shall we?

College, with its sprawling green campuses, is like a four-course meal that promises a taste of various subjects with a sprinkle of extracurricular activities. It's perfect for those who want **a broad educational experience** and perhaps aren't quite sure which career utensil to pick up yet. College comes with major expenses, but you'll get to experience a bit of everything before deciding what to major in. And let's not forget the network of friends and alumni you'll cook up—connections that can open doors down the road. **The college experience** can be a fantastic phase of your life where you build your future career and make lifelong friendships and lasting memories.

Deciding on **a college major** can feel like trying to pick a favorite ice cream flavor—there's a lot to consider, and what if you choose wrong? Start by blending your interests with potential career outcomes. Love video games? A major in computer science could lead you into game design. Fascinated by human behavior? Psychology might be your path to becoming a therapist, researcher, or consultant.

But here's a scoop: **don't just follow passion alone; sprinkle it with practicality**. Look into the future job market—is your chosen field growing or oversaturated? Will it pay enough for you to live the lifestyle you want? It's like making sure your ice cream isn't just tasty but also nourishing.

Thinking about **how to fund your education** can be as daunting as deciding who will pick up the check at a big dinner. If you are blessed with limitless funds that pay your full ride to college, congrats, my friend. That is not the norm these days, though. Start by exploring all your options: **scholarships, grants, and loans.** Scholarships and grants are the best financial aid because you don't have to pay them back—they're like the coupons of college funding. Dig around for ones you might be eligible for, from academic achievements to community service or even unique traits— yes, there are scholarships for being left-handed!

Then there's the world of **student loans**. If you go down this route, think of it as a meal plan—you'll enjoy now but pay later, likely for **a very long time**. Be wise about how much you borrow; like seasoning, a little goes a long way. And remember to apply for federal student aid by filling out the **FAFSA (Free Application for Federal Student Aid)**. It might feel like filling out a complicated recipe, but it's worth the effort. Think carefully about this because in the United States, student loans can follow you for the rest of your life, and with interest, you end up paying many times more than the initial amount of the loan.

Trade Schools and Apprenticeships

So, what happens when the traditional college route feels about as fitting as a tuxedo at a beach party? You look for alternatives that don't force you to spend four years and a fortune to get where you want to go. Enter the dynamic duo: **trade schools and apprenticeships**. These are not your backup dancers; they are the lead performers for many who want a direct path to a career without the chorus line of unrelated gen-ed courses.

Think of **trade schools** as **the express trains of education**—they get you to your destination faster, and without all the unnecessary stops. Unlike traditional universities, where you might wade through two years of history, literature, and math, trade schools drop you right into the heart of your chosen field from day one. Electrician, dental hygienist, mechanic, hairstylist, and chef are just a few of the **hands-on careers** that trade schools can prepare you for, often in two years or less. And because these programs are so **focused**, every class is relevant, making it easier to stay engaged and not feel like you're wasting time.

The cost is another huge plus. Trade schools typically come with **a much lower price tag** than four-year colleges, which means you can say goodbye to the nightmare of monstrous student debt. These schools often have strong ties to industries and can offer robust **job placement services**. This means you're getting an education and stepping into a network that can catapult you straight into employment. It's practical, it's economical, and it gets you trained and ready for specific jobs that are in demand. And let's be honest, there's something deeply satisfying about acquiring skills that allow you to build, create, and fix tangible things—it's the stuff that **job satisfaction** is made of.

Now, if you're the type who thinks that even trade school involves too much classroom time and not enough real-world action, **apprenticeships** might be your cup of tea—or your can of energy drink. Apprenticeships are all about **learning on the job**. Imagine getting hired not just to work, but to learn the ropes of a trade under the **guidance** of experienced professionals. This isn't about fetching coffee or making copies; it's about getting your hands dirty—literally or figuratively—in fields like carpentry, plumbing, or even high-tech manufacturing. Research your local trade unions and job search engines, and try **apprenticeship.gov**.

The beauty of apprenticeships is **the "earn while you learn" model**. Yes, you actually get paid to learn a trade. This means you can start building financial stability while also building a career. Plus, apprenticeships often lead to **secure jobs with good salaries and benefits**, setting you up to advance quickly. By the time your peers graduate from college, you could already be several years into a lucrative career, gaining experience and promotions. It's an option that merges education with immediate real-world application, providing a clear and direct pathway to career success without the detours.

But what if you're not ready to jump into any specific career path just yet? Maybe you need **a gap year**—a year away from traditional academic pursuits to explore other interests, travel, volunteer, or live a little before deciding what's next. While it might sound like a year-long vacation, a productive gap year is more like **a personal**

development marathon. It's about gaining skills and experiences that don't necessarily fit into a classroom but are invaluable in life and work.

A gap year can be whatever you make it. Travel abroad to teach English, volunteer with a conservation group, intern with a startup, or work a regular job to save money. The key is to **use the time to grow** in ways that will benefit you down the road. It's about expanding your worldview, building self-reliance, and possibly stumbling upon a passion that could inform your eventual career choice. Plus, colleges often view a well-spent gap year favorably as it shows maturity, initiative, and readiness to take on the challenges of higher education.

Referencing our discussions on **entrepreneurship**, remember that carving your own path by starting a business is a legitimate and potentially rewarding alternative to more structured educational paths. Whether it's turning a passion for coding into a tech startup or using culinary skills to open a food truck, entrepreneurship is about seeing opportunities and having the grit to take them. Resources, mentorship programs, and business incubators are more accessible today than ever, providing the support network necessary to launch **your own venture.**

Or, do you dream of public service where you wear a spiffy uniform while fighting crime and saving lives? Then **police work, firefighting, or the military** might be right up your alley.

Each path—trade schools, apprenticeships, gap years, entrepreneurship, public service jobs—offers unique advantages and can be tailored to fit your personal career aspirations and lifestyle choices. They're about **finding the right fit** for your personality, goals, and future vision. So, if the traditional college route feels a bit too one-size-fits-all, consider these alternatives as custom-made suits designed to fit just right, enabling you to step into the workforce with confidence, skills, and maybe even a paycheck in your hand.

Internships and Volunteering

Ah, internships and volunteering—the not-so-secret ingredients to spicing up your resume and getting a real taste of the working world. Think of them as **the ultimate trial run** for your future career, where you can test drive various roles without the long-term commitment. Plus, they are fantastic for accumulating those shiny nuggets of **experience** that make employers sit up and take notice. So, where do you start in this wide world of opportunities, and how do you ensure you stand out?

First, **finding internships** might seem like hunting for a four-leaf clover, but it's less about luck and more about knowing where to look. Start with your school's career center, which is like the treasure map to various internships—they often have partnerships with companies specifically looking for eager young minds like yours. Don't stop there; hit up job fairs, company websites, and platforms like LinkedIn or Indeed. These are not just job search engines but gateways to **potential internship goldmines**. Remember, applying for internships is like sending out invitations to a party—you want to send out a bunch to increase your chances of guests showing up!

Now, applying is one thing, but standing out is another game altogether. **Customize your application for each internship**. Yes, that means tweaking your resume and cover letter to highlight the skills and experiences that align with what they seek. Show them you've done your homework, that you know what they're about, and that you're the puzzle piece they didn't even know they were missing. **Make an impression** that says, "Hey, not only do I fit here, but I might just be the best thing that happened to this place."

Let's talk about **volunteering.** If internships are the appetizers to your career meal, volunteering is the refreshing beverage that complements any dish. It's about lending your time and skills to causes you care about, but it's also a clever way to **build professional skills.** Whether it's organizing events, managing social media pages, or helping build homes, every task adds to your skill buffet. And here's a little secret: volunteering can sometimes offer **networking opportunities** as rich as internships. You never know if the person you're planting trees with is also a manager at the tech firm you're eyeing.

But how do you make the most of these experiences? Whether it's an internship or volunteering, **building professional relationships** is crucial. Be more than just another temporary face. Engage with your colleagues, ask questions, and soak up knowledge like a sponge. Offer to help on projects outside your assigned tasks (without overloading yourself). **Show initiative,** and most importantly, **be reliable.** Nothing screams 'hire me' louder than dependability and a can-do attitude.

Finally, don't just aim to impress; aim to leave a mark. **Let your work speak for itself.** Be the intern or volunteer who does the job and does it so well that the thought of you leaving makes them want to chain you to the desk. Okay, not literally, but you get the point. And when your stint is ending, don't just fade out. Ask for feedback, request recommendations if you've really shined, and **keep those connections alive.** In today's professional world, who you know is often just as crucial as what you know.

Sweater Weather

Pivoting from your career aspirations, let's talk about change. Change is like the weather—it's unpredictable, sometimes refreshing, and other times, it hits you like a heatwave when you're wearing a winter coat. In the whirlwind of growing up and stepping into adult shoes, **the ability to adapt to change** is not just a nice skill; it's essential. Think about it: one day, you're legally a kid, and the next, you're expected to make decisions that can shape your entire future. It's like playing a video game where the levels get harder as you go, but you don't get a cheat code. So, how do you manage? You become a chameleon—mastering the art of flexibility and open-mindedness.

Flexibility is your superpower in the face of change. It means being ready to pivot and twist as life throws curveballs your way. Got a sudden shift in your college plans? Flexibility lets you explore other educational pathways without losing your cool. It means when plans change—not if, but *when*—you can **adapt** without feeling like the rug's been pulled out from under you. View change as a reroute on your GPS, not a dead end.

Open-mindedness goes hand in hand with flexibility. Be open to new experiences and ideas, even if they're outside your comfort zone. The willingness to listen and learn from diverse perspectives can broaden your horizons and spark opportunities that rigid thinking might block. Open-mindedness isn't about changing your core beliefs but **being receptive to new ideas** that could enhance your understanding and experiences.

Resilience. If life is a battle, resilience is your armor. It's what helps you bounce back from setbacks without falling apart. Building resilience starts with developing a robust **support network**—your personal cheer squad. These people lift you up when you're down, offer advice when you're stuck, and celebrate your wins no matter how small. They're your family, friends, mentors—anyone who's got your back.

A positive mindset also plays a crucial role in resilience. This is the lens through which you see challenges—as opportunities to grow rather than insurmountable obstacles. Cultivating a positive mindset involves **practicing gratitude** and focusing on what you *have* rather than what is missing. Affirm your strengths and achievements, boosting your confidence and motivating you. Remember, resilience isn't about never failing but **learning how to fail better.**

Speaking of failure, let's redefine it. Failure is not the opposite of success; it's part of it. Every misstep gives you priceless insight into what does not work, paving the way for strategies that do. **Embrace failures as stepping stones.** Analyze what went wrong, adjust your plan, and try again. You're editing a draft—the first version might be rough, but each revision brings you closer to a masterpiece.

Life is full of surprises; not all are the kind you'd celebrate. Preparing for the unexpected requires **a strategy playbook.** This includes setting up **an emergency fund** to cushion financial shocks or having **a backup plan** if your first career choice doesn't pan out. It's about being proactive rather than reactive. Contingency planning isn't pessimistic; it's smart. It ensures that you can fix the leak without panicking when life inevitably throws a wrench in your plans.

Finally, let's harness **The Four Powers** that fortify you against the winds of change.

- **First, mindfulness focus**—training your mind on the present can help manage anxiety about the future. It's about living in the now, which is the only time you can control.
- **Second, endurance to survive**—this is your ability to weather storms. It's developed through experiences that test your limits and expand your capacities.

- **Third, control over emotions**. This doesn't mean suppressing what you feel but understanding your emotions and responding to them in ways that serve you.
- **Last is powerful communication**. Articulating your thoughts and feelings effectively can help you navigate changes in relationships and environments. It ensures you're understood and that others understand you, reducing conflicts and enhancing cooperation.

As you move forward, remember that **the ability to adapt** is one of the most dynamic tools you have. It will help you turn challenges into opportunities and set the stage for continuous growth and success.

FOUR

Business is Booming

*An expert is someone called in at the last minute to share
the blame.*

Sam Ewing

So, you're ready to dive into the thrilling world of
employment, where the promises of paychecks and grown-
up responsibilities await. It's like stepping onto a giant Monopoly
board, but instead of passing Go and collecting $200, you're
crafting resumes, nailing interviews, and decoding the hiero-
glyphics on your paycheck. Let's roll the dice and get you moving
past the "Just Visiting" square.

Great Job!

Think of your **resume** as your highlight reel. It's not just a piece of
paper; it's the opening act of your career that gets your foot in the
door so you can knock their socks off in person. But as a teen,
what do you put on there? Resume **templates** are free online, so

start with your contact information (make sure your email is something like firstname.lastname@gmail.com, not crazyparty-beast2003@yahoo.com). Next, add any and all experiences that show you're **responsible and capable**: babysitting, dog walking, that summer you manned the register at your aunt's coffee shop, or the countless hours you spent organizing charity events at school.

Don't forget about **volunteer work**—it's like gold dust on a resume for someone with limited job experience. It shows you're willing to work for more than just money and commit to helping others. Also, list any skills that make you stand out. Can you code? Speak a second language? Photoshop like a pro? These are all compelling to potential employers. Finally, if you've received **any awards or recognitions**, from school or community activities, add those in. This is concrete proof that you're awesome.

Finding a job can feel like searching for a needle in a haystack—if the haystack is also moving and occasionally on fire. But don't worry, there are strategies! First, **tap into your network.** This means asking family, friends, teachers, or anyone else who might know of openings. Sometimes, getting a job is all about who you know. Next, go online. Websites like **Indeed, Glassdoor, and LinkedIn** are where many companies post listings. Also, don't forget to check local business websites, as they might list openings directly.

Make **job hunting** a regular part of your routine. Set aside weekly time to search for jobs, tailor your resume to specific roles, and send out applications. It's a numbers game, so the more you apply for, the better your chances. Remember, **persistence is key**. The job hunt can be a rollercoaster, complete with thrilling highs and disappointing lows, but staying consistent will eventually land you that first exciting role.

Congratulations, your resume caught someone's eye, and now they want to meet you! Cue the excitement—and the nerves. First, **research the company**. Showing up with knowledge about what they do and recent news or achievements is a great way to impress. Next, **practice answers** to common interview questions like, "What are your strengths and weaknesses?" or "Why do you want to work here?" Be honest, but also think about these questions ahead of time so you're not caught like a deer in headlights.

Dress for success. This doesn't mean wearing a three-piece suit (unless appropriate for the job), but wearing something tidy and professional. It shows respect for the interviewer and the job. Finally, remember to **bring a copy of your resume, a list of references, and a notebook** to jot down any thoughts or questions that might come up during the interview. Being prepared shows you're serious about the job and can give you an edge over other candidates.

So, you landed the job and now have **your first paycheck**. But wait, why does the number look different from what you expected? Let's return to the world of taxes and deductions from the previous chapter. First, understand the difference between **gross pay** (the total amount you earned before anything is taken out) and **net pay** (what actually gets deposited into your bank account). The difference is where taxes, Social Security, Medicare, and other deductions like health insurance or retirement savings come in.

It's crucial to **check your paycheck for any errors** in these deductions. Mistakes can happen and cost you money if not caught early. Also, understanding your deductions can help you budget better. Knowing exactly how much money you must spend each month is critical for financial planning. So, don't just toss **your pay stub** in a drawer; take a good look at it.

Navigating the job market as a teen can be as daunting as it is exciting but with the right tools and attitude, you can transform this challenge into a stepping stone for your future career. From crafting a standout resume to acing your interviews and understanding the fine print on your paycheck, each step is an opportunity to learn and grow

The Gig Economy

So, you've been spending countless hours on **your hobby**, be it crafting quirky jewelry, writing code that could potentially launch the next big startup, or capturing photos that even your Grandma Edna likes on Facebook. Ever thought, "Hey, could I actually make some cash from this?" Absolutely, yes! The **gig economy** isn't just for rideshare drivers or freelance graphic designers anymore. It's for anyone with a skill and the gumption to hustle, including you. Let's unpack how to turn that hobby into a **legitimate side hustle**.

First up, figure out if your hobby has the **potential to generate revenue**. Not all hobbies are marketable, but you'd be surprised how many are. Take crafting, for example. Those bracelets or custom t-shirts you make? They could be a hit on platforms like Etsy or local craft fairs. Coding, on the other hand, opens up a vast array of possibilities, from developing apps to creating websites for small businesses. And photography? Well, the world always needs more beautiful imagery for weddings, corporate events, or stock photo websites. The key here is to evaluate the demand for your hobby objectively. Look around, **see what's selling**, and identify **where you could fit into that market**. Find the intersection between doing what you love and offering something that others value.

Now, onto **the platforms that will be your launchpads**. The internet has marketplaces for almost any service or product you can imagine. Etsy is a popular choice for **handmade goods**, but don't overlook specialized platforms like ArtFire or the broader reach of eBay and Amazon Handmade. For **services** like coding or graphic design, Upwork, Freelancer, Fiverr, and Canva can connect you with clients from around the globe. Photographers can monetize their work on Shutterstock or iStock, or by setting up a professional Instagram account and attracting sponsorships. Each platform has its vibe, its rules, and its audience. Choose wisely based on where your potential customers will likely be, and **understand each platform's fee structure** and community guidelines to ensure it's a good fit for your gig.

Pricing, oh pricing — it can be the trickiest part of turning your hobby into a business. Set your prices too high, and you might scare off potential customers; too low, and you'll undervalue your work and potentially undermine the market. Start **by researching what others in your niche are charging.** This gives you a ballpark figure to work from. Next, consider the time and costs of creating your product or service. This includes direct costs like materials and indirect costs like the wear and tear on your tools. Don't forget to factor in **your time** because, yes, your time is indeed valuable. **A good pricing strategy** covers your costs, compensates you fairly for your labor, and remains attractive to customers. It's a balancing act that might take some tweaking, so be flexible and ready to adjust as you learn more about what your customers are willing to pay.

Lastly, let's talk about **customer service.** The gig economy is built on reputation. Delivering excellent customer service is essential. This means **clear communication** from the get-go, setting **realistic expectations** for delivery times, and **being responsive to inquiries** and feedback. Always aim to **exceed expectations**. Include a personal note in your shipments, offer discounts to repeat customers, or follow up to ensure they're satisfied with their purchase. When it comes to managing feedback, take the good with the bad. Positive reviews are great for business, but negative reviews can be gold if you use them to improve and resolve issues swiftly and gracefully. Remember, a happy customer is your best marketing tool; in the gig economy, word of mouth can be the wind beneath your wings.

Basics of Brand Building

When you think about brands, you might picture the heavy hitters like Apple, Nike, or even that TikTok influencer whose every post is #sponsored. But here's the inside scoop: every one of those brands started with someone defining what they stand for, their style, and how they connect with their audience. Now, it's your turn. **Building your brand** is more than slapping a cool logo on a T-shirt. You need to **craft an identity that resonates with people**, making them nod their heads and think, "Yeah, I get what this person or product is all about."

First up, **defining your brand identity**. This is like setting the stage for a rock concert where you're the headliner. What's your vibe? What values are you blasting out to the audience? Whether selling hand-crafted wallets or offering tutoring sessions, **your brand should reflect your mission and personality.** Think about what makes your offering unique. Maybe your hand-crafted wallets use environmentally friendly materials, or your tutoring sessions include game-style learning techniques that make calculus actually fun. These unique touches make your brand stand out in a sea of sameness. Remember, a well-defined brand identity attracts attention and creates loyalty. It's what keeps people coming back for your next big thing.

Now, let's talk about **wielding the power of social media** like a pro. These platforms are not just for memes and dance challenges;

they're potent tools for marketing your brand. The key? **Engagement.** Your goal is to post content that isn't just seen but interacted with. Share behind-the-scenes glimpses of your craft, tips related to your niche, or stories that stir emotions. And hey, engagement is a two-way street. Respond to comments, ask questions, and hop onto trends that align with your brand. **Each post should add value**, whether a laugh, a new idea, or a moment of inspiration. Platforms like Instagram, TikTok, and Twitter can be your best friends here, especially when you use their features to the fullest. Think Instagram Stories for quick updates or Twitter polls to get opinions. Create a community around your brand, one post at a time.

Networking might sound like something your dad does at stuffy business events, but it's about building connections that propel your brand into new territories. Start simple. Engage with peers at school, join clubs related to your interests, or attend local workshops. Each connection is a potential door to opportunities— collaborations, partnerships, or even mentorship. Online, LinkedIn can be a goldmine. **Connect with professionals** in your field, join discussions, and share your achievements. Remember, networking is about cultivating relationships that are mutually beneficial. Think of it like building a spider web where each strand strengthens your business ecosystem.

Lastly, **protecting your brand** might not sound as exciting as creating it, but it's just as crucial. Imagine this: you've built a killer brand, only to find someone else cashing in on your hard work. Not cool, right? This is where understanding the basics of **intellectual property** comes in. *Trademarks* **protect brand names and logos**, while *copyrights* **protect creative works**. It's like putting a shield around your empire.

You might not need to file for protection immediately, but knowing how these laws work can save you from headaches down the line. Go to the **U.S. Copyright Office** online and the **U.S. Patent and Trademark Office**. Simple steps like the ™ symbol can assert your claim, giving you some muscle in the legal gym.

Building your brand is like crafting your legend in the marketplace. It's about standing out, connecting authentically, and protecting your creative turf. As you weave these elements together, your brand starts to live not just in your products or services but in the hearts of your audience. It becomes a story they want to be part of, a community they trust, and a name they champion.

Your Side Hustle Elevator Pitch

Imagine you're stuck in an elevator with the one person who could rocket your business into the stratosphere. You've got maybe 30 seconds to turn their world upside down (in a good way), to pitch your idea so compellingly that by the time those doors glide open, they're begging for your business card. That, my friend, **is the power of an effective elevator pitch**. It's your business in a nutshell, delivered quickly enough to be heard between floors but memorable enough to stick with them all day.

So, what makes an elevator pitch not just good but great? It starts with **clarity**. Your pitch should be a laser-focused beam of information. No rambling. Every word counts. Begin with a hook—*a problem your business solves in a way no one else can*. Maybe your handmade skateboards use recycled materials, appealing to eco-conscious skaters, or your tutoring app uses AI to adapt lessons to each student's pace. That **hook** is your headline, your foot in the door. Follow up with the stakes. Why does it matter? Maybe those skateboards are saving truckloads of waste from landfills, or your app could revolutionize learning for students with learning disabilities. This isn't just your business plan; it's your battle cry.

Then, paint a picture of the outcome. **What does success look like, thanks to your product or service?** Perhaps it's a world where learning is so personalized that no student ever feels left behind. Or maybe you're creating a new culture of sustainability in the skating community. This vision is what you sell; not just a product, but a future. Wrap up with what you need to make it happen—maybe funding, advice, or connections. This isn't begging; it's inviting them to be part of your story. And always, always end with **a call to action**: "Can I send you an email with more details?" "Could we grab a coffee to discuss this further?" Make it easy for them to say yes.

But here's the thing: not every elevator ride is with a potential investor or a business guru. Sometimes, it's with a potential first customer, a mentor, or partner. That's why **tailoring your pitch** is as crucial as the pitch itself. Think of it like choosing the right filter for your selfie; you want to highlight your best features based on who's looking. If you're talking to a tech expert, beef up the tech aspects of your app. Chatting with an environmental activist? Emphasize the sustainable angle of your materials. The core of your pitch stays the same, but the focus shifts based on who's listening.

This **customization** means you need to *know your audience*. What drives them? What do they value? Your goal is to connect on a level that resonates deeply with their world. It's empathy in action. You're showing that you understand and share their concerns and that your business isn't just selling a product or service—it's **solving a problem** they care about. This doesn't mean you need a dozen different pitches. Often, just tweaking a few key phrases and focusing on different aspects of your value proposition can shift the entire tone to suit your audience better.

Now, let's talk about **practice.** Because let's face it, even the most well-crafted pitch can crash and burn if delivered with the enthusiasm of soggy toast. **Your delivery** needs to be as sharp as your message. This means practice and then more practice. Start in front of a mirror. Watch your facial expressions and body language. Are you conveying confidence? Excitement? Passion? These visual cues are as much a part of your pitch as the words you choose.

Then, level up to **recording yourself**. It might feel awkward, but it's the fastest way to catch those ums and uhs, those rambling sentences that dilute your message, or that nervous laughter that sneaks in unexpectedly. Play it back, critique it, and do it again. Once you've got that down, **start pitching to friends or family**. They'll offer feedback that a mirror can't, like whether your message is as clear as you think or if your energy is more 'deflated balloon' than a 'firework.' The goal here is muscle memory. You want the words to come out naturally, leaving your brain free to adapt on the fly and engage with your listener.

Finally, **propel yourself out there** as much as possible. Networking events are classic pitching grounds but don't limit yourself. That coffee shop chat with a friend of a friend, the quick exchange at a community event, or even an online forum can be the perfect place to deploy your pitch. The key is to keep it natural. If someone asks, "What do you do?" That's your opening. Slide in your pitch as a natural part of the conversation. It shouldn't feel like a commercial break; it should be a seamless part of the dialogue that leaves them wanting more.

Always be ready. Keep business cards or a digital portfolio handy to capitalize on the interest you've sparked. And remember, each pitch is a mini-performance. The more you do it, the better you get. So keep pitching, keep refining, and keep riding those elevators. Who knows who you'll meet on your next ride up?

Funding Your Dream

Starting a business can feel like being a superhero in a comic book —you've got the vision and the drive, but you're still figuring out how to finance your superpowers. This is where mastering the art of budgeting and understanding funding options comes into play, transforming you from a dreamer into a doer.

First off, let's talk **budgeting**. It's not just about keeping tabs on your cash flow; you'll need **strategic planning** to ensure your business doesn't go belly up before it gets off the ground. Start by **separating your personal finances from your business finances**. This is crucial! You don't want your personal Netflix subscription messing up your business accounts, right? Open a business bank account and use it *exclusively* for business transactions. This will save you a mountain of headaches when tax season rolls around.

Now, onto creating your budget. **List all possible expenses**— materials, marketing, rent, website hosting, and yes, even your salary. Then, **forecast** your expected income. Be realistic. It's better to underestimate your income and overestimate your expenses. This way, you won't find yourself in a financial pickle. **Track everything**. Use budgeting tools or **apps** specifically designed for small businesses to keep a tight rein on your finances. This ongoing process helps you see where you're bleeding money and where you can maybe tighten up or splurge a bit.

Making a profit is exhilarating, but what do you do with that money? **Reinvesting profits** back into your business is crucial for growth. However, you have to be smart about it. Don't just throw cash at every problem or shiny new tool. You need to **prioritize**. Maybe that advanced course in digital marketing could bring more ROI (return on investment) than a fancy new office chair. Or perhaps investing in better equipment will speed up your production time, allowing you to serve more customers.

The key is **balance**. You want to reinvest enough to fuel growth, but not so much that you're running your reserves dry. It's like watering a plant: Too little water and it wilts; too much and it drowns. Find that sweet spot where your investments nurture your business without overwhelming it.

You'll likely need external funding unless you've found a tree that grows money. There are several routes you can explore. **Bootstrapping** is starting with your own money and growing through incoming revenues. It's tough but rewarding, as it keeps you debt-free. If bootstrapping sounds like a slow burn, consider a **small business loan**. Local banks and online lenders offer various options but read the fine print. Understand the interest rates and repayment terms before you sign anything.

Grants are another fantastic funding source, especially because you don't have to pay them back. Look for local government or private grants aimed at young entrepreneurs. Then there's **crowdfunding**—platforms like Kickstarter or Indiegogo where you pitch your business idea to the world, and anyone interested can contribute funding. It's also a great way to gauge interest in your product or service.

Finally, **setting financial goals** creates the roadmap for your business finances. Start with short-term goals, like achieving a certain sales target by the end of the quarter or reducing production costs by 10%. These are your stepping stones. Then, outline your long-term goals. Maybe you see your business scaling to a national level or diversifying into new markets. These goals are your horizon—what you're ultimately aiming for.

Each financial goal should be **SMART: Specific, Measurable, Achievable, Relevant, and Time-bound**. This framework outlines what you want to achieve and how and when. Regularly review and adjust your goals as your business grows and evolves. It's a dynamic process, much like navigating a ship. You need to adjust your sails (always keep adapting!) as the winds of the business world change

FIVE

Relationships: Keep Talking

> *I didn't mean to push all your buttons. I was just looking for mute.*
>
> @rebel circus

Mastering the art of conversation demands a delicate balance of timing, wit, and a flair for the unexpected. Beyond the words, it's the rhythm you create—a symphony of dialogue where every nuance plays its part. So, sharpen your verbal dexterity and soon you'll be transforming every chat into a meaningful connection, whether a deep heart-to-heart or a light, breezy dialogue.

The Art of Conversation: Listen

Let's kick things off with **active listening**, which, contrary to popular belief, involves much more than just nodding at regular intervals while secretly planning your next snack. Active listening fully engages with the person speaking, giving them the stage without interruptions. It means tuning into their words with your ears, eyes, and heart. Make eye contact—it tells the speaker they are the most interesting person in the room. And here's a pro tip: throw in a few verbal acknowledgments like "I see" or "Interesting," and watch the conversation deepen. This is more than politeness; it **shows genuine interest and builds trust**. It lets the speaker know you're not just waiting for your turn to talk; you're really with them, in that moment, for every word. If you're mentally rehearsing your reply as they speak, you're not really listening.

Now, onto the flip side—**expressing yourself**. Ever played the game of telephone, where "I like cats" turns into "Eileen eats bats"? That's what happens when we don't express ourselves clearly. To keep your words from being lost in translation, *use "I" statements*. Simple yet profound "I" statements allow you to convey your thoughts and feelings without sounding accusatory. For instance, instead of saying, "You never listen," try, "I feel overlooked when you check your phone while I'm talking." See the shift? It's less about blame and more about **your feelings**, which opens up the conversation rather than shutting it down.

Questions are the secret sauce that keeps the conversation flowing. But not just any questions—**open-ended questions**. These questions can't be answered with a simple yes or no. They require thought and elaboration, which means they are fantastic for digging deeper. Swap "Did you like the movie?" with "What did you think about the movie?" The first might get you a "It was fine," while the second opens up a whole world of discussion. Questions like these show that you're not just making conversation; you're interested in the other person's opinions and thoughts. They turn a simple exchange into a **dialogue**, a chance to explore and connect.

Here's the not-so-fun part—**difficult conversations**. They're like the boss level in video games; they require all your skills and a cool head. The key to navigating these tricky waters is staying calm and looking for **common ground**. Suppose you're debating a sensitive topic. It's easy to get heated, but remember, the goal isn't to win; it's to understand and to be understood. Focus on **what you agree on**, not just where you differ. This doesn't mean you water down your beliefs; rather, you're seeking a bridge, not a barrier. And sometimes, **agreeing to disagree** is the bridge. The goal is to respect each other's views enough to allow space for them, which can sometimes be the most productive outcome of all.

Emotional Intelligence: Yes, Please

Emotional Intelligence (**EI**) is not just another buzzword floating around self-help gurus; it's the real MVP when it comes to navigating the emotional rollercoaster known as your teen years. Picture EI as your internal toolkit for managing your emotions and those around you. Let's start with **self-awareness**, the cornerstone of EI. It's like being the Sherlock Holmes of your own emotions. It is crucial to understand what you feel, why you feel it, and how it affects your actions. This isn't about suppressing your feelings but recognizing them and **understanding their impact** on your actions and decisions. For instance, realizing that you're not just cranky, you're stressed because of an upcoming exam can shift your response from snapping at your friends to taking a few deep breaths or planning a study schedule. It requires **observing your emotional responses** like a scientist—curious, detached, and always learning.

Empathy is about stepping into someone else's shoes, except you're not taking their shoes; you're understanding their feelings. Empathy goes beyond feeling sorry for someone. This is genuinely understanding their experiences and emotions from their perspective. It's **seeing the world through their eyes.** When your friend is upset because they bombed a test, empathy allows you to feel their disappointment, not just acknowledge it. This doesn't mean you drown in their sadness; instead, it helps you connect with them on a deeper level, which can strengthen your relationships like crazy glue.

EI really comes into play when **managing emotions, especially intense ones like anger or frustration.** Think of it as emotional judo—you're using your awareness of your emotions to master them, not fight them. **Techniques** like deep breathing, counting to ten, or channeling your frustrations into physical activities like sports or even a fast-paced walk can work wonders. The goal is not to bottle up these feelings but to find healthy outlets for them. For instance, write it down instead of lashing out when you're infuriated. Express what you feel on paper. This helps to cool down your emotional engine so you don't end up saying or doing things you might regret.

Last but certainly not least, **improving your social skills** is another crucial aspect of EI. This doesn't mean becoming the life of the party; it's knowing how to interact comfortably in various social settings. This includes **reading non-verbal cues** like body language and facial expressions, which can often tell you more about how someone feels than their words. For example, if someone is crossing their arms and looking away while you're talking, they might not just be cold but disinterested or uncomfortable. **Adjusting your approach** based on these cues can make you a more effective communicator. Also, **adapting to different social situations** is key. How you chat with your BFF about a new movie differs from how you discuss your project ideas with your teacher. Understanding these **social nuances** and adjusting your behavior accordingly can make your social interactions smoother and more productive, like oiling the gears of your social machinery.

Shameless Plug alert! If you want to take a fun dive into Emotional Intelligence, relationships, and navigating your life path, get my book *Mindful Numerology: Your Guide to Emotional Awareness, Personal Fulfillment, and Deeper Relationships.* It's a real spiritual and psychological trip!

When you develop these aspects of Emotional Intelligence, you not only enhance your personal relationships but also set up a strong foundation for handling professional interactions in the future. It's about building a robust emotional skill set to help you navigate life's ups and downs more smoothly. So, keep honing these skills, and watch as they transform your interactions one conversation at a time, making you not just emotionally intelligent but emotionally wise.

Setting Boundaries: Respect Yourself

Imagine you're the director of your own life's movie. You get to call the shots on who enters your personal space, how they can interact with you, and when it's time for them to exit stage left. This is about understanding and **establishing your personal boundaries**, essential for maintaining your well-being and healthy relationships. Think of boundaries like **the rules of a game**; everyone knows what's expected, and everyone plays better because of them. They help you **respect yourself** and train others to do the same, ensuring every relationship is built on **mutual respect.**

So, how do you start drawing these invisible lines? First, you must determine **where you stand on various issues**—what you're okay with and what makes you want to run for the hills. It's like setting

your privacy settings on social media; some things you're cool sharing, and some things are just for you. This can range from **your
comfort level** with physical touch, like hugs, to how much personal
info you want to share in a conversation. Identifying these boundaries is a personal journey—what works for your best friend might
not work for you, which is totally fine. Reflect on past experiences:
when did you feel uncomfortable, and why? What made you feel
safe and respected? These reflections can be **your guideposts.**

Now comes the tricky part—**communicating these boundaries.**
It's not just about being honest; it's about being **clear and firm,**
without being defensive or apologetic. For instance, if you're not a
fan of last-minute plans, tell your friends straightforwardly: "I
really value our time together, but I need a heads-up at least a day
in advance to manage my schedule." It's **straightforward** and
respectful. Remember, setting boundaries is not a one-time deal.
This is an **ongoing process of defining and articulating your
limits clearly and respectfully,** ensuring those around you understand your needs and expectations.

But it's not just about setting your boundaries; it's also about
respecting others. **We teach people how to treat us.** Just as you
want your limits to be acknowledged, you need to accept and
honor the boundaries others set with you. This **reciprocal respect**
makes interactions smoother and relationships more enjoyable. If
a friend says they need some alone time, resist the urge to take it
personally or bombard them with messages. By showing respect
for their needs, you strengthen the trust and respect in your relationship and **set a standard** for how you expect to be treated in
return.

Navigating the landscape of personal boundaries helps prevent
feelings of resentment or discomfort, making your social interac-

tions more fulfilling and less stressful. It's about giving yourself permission to put your well-being first and **empowering** those around you to do the same. So, as you continue to interact and grow within your relationships, keep these boundary basics in mind—they're not just guidelines but the building blocks for healthy, respectful, and enjoyable interactions with friends, family, and beyond.

Navigating Family Dynamics

Family—the folks you share DNA with but sometimes wonder if the lab made a mistake. Kidding aside, navigating the shifting sands of family relationships can be like trying to solve a Rubik's Cube blindfolded. As you morph from a teen into a full-fledged adult, **family roles inevitably transform**, and so does your part in the grand family play. Originally, you might have been the understudy, the kid who followed the script—do your homework, clean your room, be home by curfew. But as you edge into adulthood, you're more like a co-director in your life drama. You start making more decisions, from the mundane (like choosing your own clothes) to the major (like picking a career path). This shift can be liberating, but it can also cause a bit of friction, especially if your family's still reading from the old script.

Here's where flexing your communication muscles becomes crucial. Imagine you're negotiating a treaty. You want to maintain peace and foster goodwill, right? The same goes for family discussions. When roles are changing, **clear communication** is your best ally. Explain your viewpoint, new needs, and boundaries clearly and respectfully. Yes, respect. It's a two-way street. Just as you desire more autonomy, **recognize the concerns** your family might have about this new dynamic. They're not just being overprotective; they're adjusting to the new you, just as you're adjusting to a more grown-up you.

Let's talk about the elephant in the room: **family conflict**. It's inevitable. Conflict is often rooted in misunderstanding or miscommunication, whether it's bickering over chores or clashing over curfews. Here's a pro strategy: instead of gearing up for battle, **try to understand** where the other person is coming from. Maybe your mom nags about your messy room because she's stressed about guests coming over. Or perhaps your dad's strict curfew is because he worries about your safety. When you approach conflicts with a detective's curiosity rather than a gladiator's aggression, you're more likely to find a solution that works for everyone. And remember, the goal is not to win; it's to **resolve and strengthen the bond**.

Changes in **family structure** are another layer in this complex cake. Whether it's dealing with divorce, welcoming a stepparent, or moving to a new city, each scenario demands a bucket load of adaptability. Take divorce, for example. It can feel like your family puzzle has been thrown into the air, and you're left grabbing at pieces. Here, maintaining open lines of communication with both parents is key. **Express your feelings** about the changes, but be open to hearing their side of the story. With remarriage, **give yourself time to adjust** to the new family member. It's okay if you don't feel instant connections; relationships **take time to build**. If a move is in the cards, focus on the positives. New place, new experiences, new friends. It's like hitting the refresh button on your social life, albeit a bit daunting.

Finally, amidst all these changes and challenges, keeping the family connection alive is like ensuring your phone's plugged into the power bank. You want that green light, that full charge. **Find ways to stay connected** as you carve out your path toward independence. Schedule regular family game nights, have meals together, or simply share details about your day. These moments act as glue, strengthening the family bond even as you enjoy your independence. Plus, it reminds you that no matter how grown-up you get, there's a squad back home who's always got your back.

Healthy Friendships: Resolving Conflicts

Let's face it, friendships are like your own personal sitcom—sometimes you're laughing together, and sometimes you're navigating the plot twists that life throws at you. But what makes a friendship really stick through the seasons? It's built on a foundation of **trust, respect, and mutual support**. Imagine having a friend who cheers you on when you score the winning goal and passes you tissues and binge-watches movies with you post-breakup. This kind of friendship isn't just about sharing hobbies or history; it's about providing a **safe space** where you feel **valued and supported**, where secrets aren't broadcasted and private jokes aren't explained.

Now, flip the script, and let's chat about those friendships that feel more like a mystery thriller than a comfy sitcom. Yep, we're talking about **toxic relationships**. They can be sneaky, starting off as perfect until the plot thickens with manipulation or disrespect. Maybe it's that friend who only texts when they need homework answers or the one who subtly puts you down with "just kidding" digs. **Recognizing these red flags** is crucial. A friendship should not feel like a constant battle for respect or a one-way street of favors. It's about balance and mutual respect, where both give and take are equal and *where your victories are celebrated, not envied.*

When conflicts arise—and they will because, spoiler alert, no friendship is perfect—the handling counts. Think of **conflict resolution** as a dance. You want to move together, not step on each other's toes. Start by keeping the lines of communication open. **Address issues directly** instead of letting them simmer and potentially boil over. For instance, if a friend repeatedly bails on plans, instead of brewing resentment, have a chat. Maybe they're overbooked or facing personal issues. Understanding the full picture can transform frustration into compassion. And when discussing the issue, aim for **a win-win resolution** where both sides feel heard and valued rather than a win-lose scenario where one of you walks away feeling defeated.

But what about when a friendship **feels beyond repair?** Sometimes, despite your best efforts, the healthiest option is to **let go.** Ending a friendship can feel like pulling off a Band-Aid—quick and painful—but it's often necessary for personal growth and well-being. Recognizing when a relationship is detracting more than adding to your life is important. If interactions consistently leave you feeling **drained, undervalued, or disrespected**, it's time to reevaluate. Approaching this situation requires honesty and tact. Express your feelings clearly and respectfully, without blame or bitterness. A simple "I think our friendship isn't as healthy as it could be, and I need to step back" (remember to use 'I' statements) acknowledges the issue without escalating emotions. You want to protect your well-being, not create drama. By **handling the situation with dignity**, you preserve your self-respect and leave the door open for possible future reconciliation, should circumstances change.

Navigating the complexities of friendships—from fostering healthy dynamics to recognizing when it's time to walk away— requires **emotional intelligence, communication skills, and, sometimes, tough decisions.** But through these interactions, you learn more about yourself, others, and the types of relationships that help you thrive. So, cherish the good moments, learn from the challenges, and don't be afraid to stand up for the respect you deserve. After all, the friends who truly matter are those who grow with you, not those you outgrow.

The Dating Game

Ah, the dating game—a mix of thrilling moments, awkward silences, and sometimes, butterflies that could rival a wildlife documentary. But beyond the fun and often comedic misadventures lies the serious business of **understanding and practicing consent**, which is the cornerstone of any healthy relationship. Consider consent not just a formal agreement but a mutual, enthusiastic, and **continuous conversation about comfort levels and boundaries**. It's about ensuring that every step, every touch, and every word is agreed upon by both parties. This means having clear and honest communication where "yes" means yes, and *anything less* than an enthusiastic yes—be it a hesitant 'maybe' or a non-committal 'um, okay'—is a no.

Navigating this terrain requires you to **be both bold and respectful**. Bold in expressing what you're comfortable with and what you're not, and respectful in understanding and accepting your partner's boundaries without question or persuasion. **Consent should be as clear as a sunny day.** If you're in doubt, it's a signal to pause and talk it out. Healthy relationships require **hard conversations**. It's not about killing the mood; it's about enhancing trust and respect, which, believe it or not, can actually make the relationship stronger and more intimate.

Building a healthy relationship is like planting a garden. It requires time, effort, and a lot of TLC (tender, loving care, not the '90s girl group, though they're awesome too). A key ingredient? **Maintaining your individuality.** Yes, being part of a couple doesn't mean you morph into one person. Keep up with your hobbies, maintain your friendships, and have your own opinions.

These elements bring vibrancy to your life and richness to your conversations. They keep the relationship fresh and exciting because **you both bring unique experiences** to the table every day. And remember, **mutual respect** is non-negotiable. This means listening to each other, valuing each other's opinions, and supporting each other's ambitions. It's about cheering for each other in successes and offering a shoulder or an ice cream tub during the lows.

Navigating **dating apps** is emotionally, mentally, and physically challenging because it's a jungle out there. Here are some tips to keep in mind as you read profiles: Pay close attention to **the language** the person uses in describing themselves and what they look for in a partner. If anything they say makes you vaguely **uncomfortable,** yet you can't quite focus on why, that is an automatic swipe left or block. Often they are telling you what **you** need to do for them and how **you** need to look or behave, which is not an emotionally healthy approach. **Trust your gut** and move on.

After you do go on a date with someone, **ask yourself a few questions:**

- *Did you feel relaxed and comfortable in their presence?*
- *Did they bring out a happy, fun side of you?*
- *Did they make you laugh?*
- *Did you get a good feeling from their energy that kept you interested and curious about them?*

Your **intuition** knows what is right for you, so please don't be in any rush to make something work if you are just not feeling it or if you feel uneasy about any aspect of the date.

But what happens when things don't work out? **Handling breakups** with dignity and respect is crucial. It's recognizing that just because the relationship is ending, your **respect** for each other doesn't have to. Take the high road. **Communicate openly** about why things are not working, and avoid the blame game. **Focus on self-healing and growth.** This might involve soul-searching, reconnecting with friends, or diving into activities that make you feel good about yourself. Allow yourself **time to grieve** the relationship and recognize when it's time to move forward. You can't erase the past but you can learn from it and use those lessons to enrich your future relationships.

Lastly, amidst the whirlwind of dating and relationships, don't forget to **enjoy your youth.** This is a time for discovery—about the world, others, and most importantly, yourself. There is no rush to jump into serious relationships if you're not ready. Explore, have fun, and **take your time.** Dating should be about **finding out what you want** in a partner and enjoying the company of people who make you laugh and feel valued, not pressured to conform to some timeline or societal expectation.

So, as you navigate the dating scene, remember to communicate clearly, respect boundaries, maintain your individuality, handle breakups with maturity, and enjoy the process of meeting new people and learning more about yourself. These experiences are not just about finding a partner but about enriching your understanding of connecting deeply with another person.

SIX

Let's Get Digital

> *Before you marry a person, you should first make them use a computer with slow internet to see who they really are.*
>
> Will Ferrell

Welcome to the digital jungle! It's wild and chaotic, and where your digital footprint can either be a path to opportunities or a trail of breadcrumbs leading trouble right to your doorstep. Think of the internet as a tattoo parlor; what goes online stays online, often forever. Like a tattoo, your digital actions are there for the world to see, and removing them can be... well, more painful than getting inked in the first place. So, let's navigate through the pixels and URLs to ensure your digital footprint is more like a work of art than a regrettable late-night decision.

The Permanent Internet

Every tweet you tweet, every status you update, every picture you post, and even every page you thumb through on the web leaves digital footprints. These **footprints** create a portrait of who you are online, which can be seen by friends, family, and sometimes, the entire world—including potential employers or colleges. It's like leaving a paper trail, except it's not paper; it's made of bits and bytes and a lot harder to erase.

So, why should you care? Well, these footprints can have **long-term impacts**. Positive footprints, like posts about your volunteer work or achievements, can open doors by showcasing your best self. Negative ones, like inappropriate photos or offensive comments, can slam those doors shut. Plus, your online behavior can affect your digital reputation, just like offline behavior affects your personal reputation.

Laws like the General Data Protection Regulation (GDPR) in the EU and the California Consumer Privacy Act (CCPA) in the U.S. have been enacted **to protect your privacy** and ensure the internet doesn't turn into the Wild West. These laws are like the internet's version of a privacy shield, giving you rights over your data. They make sure companies are transparent about what data they are collecting on you and why and **give you the power** to ask for your data to be deleted. It is akin to having a magic eraser for your digital footprints, at least with companies that hold your information.

Before you hit 'share' on that next post, pause, ask yourself, and sometimes ask others, "Is this okay?" **Consent** in the digital world is just as important as it is in the real world. Whether you're tagging friends in photos or sharing someone else's post, getting a thumbs-up from everyone involved is crucial. It respects their privacy and can save you from potential headaches down the line. Remember, once something is out there, it's out of your control.

Just like you wouldn't leave your window shades open all the time, don't leave your digital windows uncovered. Dive into the **privacy settings** on your social media platforms. It's like setting up curtains and deciding who gets to peek inside. These settings control who can see your posts, who can tag you, and even who can comment. Customize them to suit your comfort level. It might seem tedious, but it's essential for maintaining **your digital sanctuary**.

Here's a rule of thumb: If you wouldn't shout it out loud in a crowded room, maybe don't post it online. Every share, like, or comment should pass **the "future regret" test**. Think about how it could be perceived in the future. This isn't just about avoiding embarrassment but protecting your privacy and reputation. A moment of pause can be the difference between a post that enhances your reputation and one that tarnishes it.

Just like you would clean your room (hopefully), take time to **clean up your digital space**. This means going through your social media profiles and removing anything that doesn't represent who you are or who you want to be in the future. Like tidying up your room before you have guests over, you want to put your best foot forward. Start by reviewing your old posts, photos, and even likes. If it doesn't fit your current or desired image, it might be **time for it to go**.

Navigating your digital life can be as tricky as walking a tightrope, but with the right knowledge and tools, you can ensure your digital footprint is safe and positive. Think of it as curating an online museum of yourself, one that you'd be proud to show off. Just keep thinking critically about the digital image you craft.

Cybersecurity Guard

Welcome to your new role as a Cybersecurity Guard—think of it as being the superhero of your own online universe, where villains are hackers and innocent citizens are your personal data. First up, let's talk about the foundation of all online security: **passwords.** Creating a strong, unique password is like building a high-tech fortress around your digital life. Forget your pet's name followed by 123; we're talking about passwords that could take centuries to crack. You already know to mix it up with upper and lowercase letters, numbers, and symbols. Think of something you can remember, but others can't guess. Maybe a **random sentence** like, "My2Cats!Love2Fish@Lake-Wakaboo." Weird but effective!

Now, managing these passwords doesn't mean jotting them down on sticky notes around your computer. Use a reputable **password manager**. These are the secret vaults that not only store your passwords securely but often generate those almost uncrackable passwords for you. And whenever you can, turn on **two-factor authentication (2FA)**. It adds an extra layer of security by requiring not just your password but also something only you have on you, like your smartphone. It's like having a second lock on your door.

Moving on to phishing—no, not the one with a rod and bait, but the kind that's a major headache in the cyber world. **Phishing** attempts are sneaky efforts by scammers to trick you into giving up personal information. They might send you an email that looks like it's from your bank, complete with logos and official language, but is actually as fake as a three-dollar bill. They'll urge you to click a link and log in to a page that looks legit but is actually a copy designed to steal your credentials. The golden rule here? **Don't do it!** Never click on links from emails or messages that you weren't expecting. Always double-check by going directly to the website by typing it into your browser or calling the company directly.

Safe browsing is another critical skill in your cybersecurity tool-kit. Stick to reputable websites, particularly those **with 'https' in the URL, which indicates they are secure.** Watch out for sites that bombard you with too many pop-ups or ask for unnecessary personal information. Installing a good **antivirus program** is also like having a loyal guard dog—it can alert you to dangers before they harm you. Make sure it's always updated to keep up with the new tricks hackers might throw at you.

Lastly, let's talk about keeping your software and apps up to date. I know, those **update notifications** always seem to pop up at the most inconvenient times, like when you're right in the middle of beating your high score. But these updates don't just add new features; they're often patching up security holes that hackers could exploit. Ignoring updates is like having a broken window in your fortress and thinking, "Oh, it'll be fine." Spoiler: it won't. Set your devices to **update automatically overnight**, so you wake up safer every day without having to lift a finger.

Social Media Smarts: Get Happy

Navigating the labyrinth of social media is like steering a space-ship through an asteroid belt—thrilling, a bit risky, and totally worth it if you know what you're doing. Let's start with **curating your online persona**. Don't just slap together a profile with your favorite selfie and a quirky bio. You want to craft an image that reflects your genuine self, your values, and where you see your future self heading. This is your **personal brand**. Every tweet, every share, and every comment contributes to this brand. You're painting a mural of yourself, one brushstroke at a time, for the world to see. So, before you post, ask yourself, does this fit the 'mural' I'm creating? Is it a true reflection of my beliefs and aspirations? This could mean sharing achievements that align with your career goals, posts that reflect your commitment to social issues, or just content that highlights your hobbies and interests. **Be intentional** with what you share to ensure it reflects the 'you' that you want the world to see.

Now, let's talk about impact—specifically, the **impact of social media on your mental health** and real-life relationships. It's no secret that while social media can be a great way to stay connected, it can also be a breeding ground for stress, anxiety, and **FOMO** (fear of missing out). Seeing everyone's highlight reels can make your own life feel less exciting. But remember that what's shared on social media is often a curated version of reality. It's the triumphs without the trials, the success without the struggle. So, take what you see with a grain of salt and remember it's not a competition. Instead, focus on using social media to uplift your spirits. Follow accounts that **inspire you**, share content that makes you feel good, and **engage positively** with others. Make your feed a source of inspiration rather than frustration, and watch as your online world becomes **a happier place**, reflecting positively on your real-life relationships as well.

Moving onto **networking**—social media isn't just for memes and cat videos (though they truly brighten my day!); it's a powerful tool for **building your professional future**. As we discussed earlier, platforms like LinkedIn can be goldmines for connecting with industry professionals, joining groups related to your career interests, and finding job opportunities. But other platforms like Twitter and Instagram are also valuable. You can follow companies you're interested in, engage with their posts, and even get noticed by potential employers through your insightful comments and shares. Treat each interaction as a mini-interview; you never know who might be watching. Share content that is **relevant to your**

field, comment thoughtfully, and build a network that reflects where you want your career path to go.

Finally, let's detox—digitally. Yes, social media can be addictive. It's designed to keep you scrolling, liking, and consuming without end. But like any good thing, **moderation is key**. Regular **digital detoxes** can help you reset and recharge. This doesn't mean you must go full hermit and shun all digital devices. Rather, **take intentional breaks**—maybe during dinner, an hour before bed, or even a full day over the weekend. Use this time to connect with friends and family in person, read a book, or dive into a hobby. Notice how **your stress levels drop** and your real-world interactions become more meaningful. Give your brain a little vacation, a break from the constant bombardment of information and notifications. And when you return to the digital world, you'll likely find that you haven't missed much and might even feel more in control of your interactions.

Online Relationships: Red Flags

Navigating the intricate web of online relationships is like playing a multiplayer video game—sometimes, you team up with awesome players, and other times, you encounter trolls who can turn the experience sour. The key to maintaining a healthy online rapport is distinguishing between behavior that **uplifts you** and behavior that drags you down. Just like in real life, a healthy online relationship is **based on mutual respect, trust, and open communication**. It should make you feel supported, not stifled. It's cool when someone likes your posts or texts you to check in, but it crosses into unhealthy territory when they demand to know your password or constantly monitor whom you're chatting with. This type of controlling behavior is a glaring red flag. **Setting boundaries** that protect your sense of freedom and privacy is crucial.

Speaking of **red flags**, they can sometimes be tricky to spot, especially when you're enjoying the attention someone gives you online. However, **certain signs** should immediately have you on high alert. For instance, if someone is overly possessive, frequently demanding your time to the point where it feels suffocating, it's a signal that the relationship might not be as wholesome as it appears. Another significant red flag is if they ask for **personal details** early on—like your home address, daily schedule, or even financial information. Do not do it! These queries are not just nosy; they're potentially dangerous. **Decline these requests without explanation or apology.** Whether platonic or romantic, online relationships should progress at a pace that feels comfortable and safe for you. Anyone pushing too fast for personal details is not seeking your best interests.

Now, let's chat about privacy and **sharing**. In the digital age, sharing is just a click away, but not every piece of information should be shared. Does everyone need to know what flavor yogurt you had for lunch? Protecting your privacy online means **being selective** about what you share on public platforms. Even something as simple as your birthday or the school you attend can be used against you for identity theft or to hack into your accounts. Before you share, think about who might see this information and how it could be used. A good practice is to **review your privacy settings regularly** to ensure you only share information with people you trust. Furthermore, be **cautious about whom you add as a friend or follower**. If you wouldn't trust them with a key to your house, why let them into the virtual rooms of your online world?

Lastly, if an online interaction makes you feel uncomfortable, unsafe, or pressured, **it's important to seek help.** Don't go through it alone. Talk to a trusted adult or a friend or contact an online support group. Many websites and social platforms have reporting tools that allow you to **report abusive behavior**. Use them. No one has the right to make you feel threatened or harassed online. Remember, blocking someone who makes you feel unsafe is self-care, and often, it's necessary to maintain your mental and emotional health. Being proactive about whom you interact with and how you manage these interactions can empower you to **cultivate a healthier, happier online environment**. So keep these red flags in mind, set your **boundaries** firmly, and continue enjoying the vast, dynamic world of online socializing with confidence and caution.

The Dark Spider Web

Online scams are just one piece of the puzzle. The digital world also has its bullies, known as **cyberbullies.** These aren't your playground bullies; they're more insidious, using texts and social media to harass or embarrass. If you find yourself targeted, know **it's not your fault and you're not alone.** Cyberbullying can leave deep emotional scars, and dealing with it head-on is crucial. First, *do not engage.* Responding can sometimes fuel the fire. Instead, document the abuse. Take screenshots and save messages. They serve as **evidence** if you decide to report the issue. Most social platforms have straightforward methods for reporting harassment, and schools often have protocols for handling cyberbullying.

Critical thinking is your best defense when consuming information online. The internet is awash with **misinformation**, from slightly skewed facts to outright fabrications. Always cross-check news from multiple reputable sources before accepting it as true. Look for red flags like sensational headlines or articles lacking credible sources. **Developing a critical eye** can help you sift fact from fiction and make you a smarter, more aware internet user.

Remember, the internet is a tool, and like any tool, how you use it can either build or break. You can **navigate the digital world safely and confidently** by staying informed about scams, protecting yourself from cyberbullying, guarding your personal information, and thinking critically about the information you consume. Keep these strategies in mind as you explore the vast online universe, ensuring your journey is enriching and secure.

SEVEN

Just Take a Nap

I generally avoid temptation unless I can't resist it.

Mae West

Healthy habits...You start off with the best intentions, stocking your fridge with kale and signing up for a gym membership with all the enthusiasm of a kid on Christmas morning. But then life happens, and suddenly you're hitting snooze on your morning run and reaching for the cookies instead of the carrots. You tell yourself you're going to tackle your stress with a deeply Zen yoga session, but you can't find your other sneaker, and this great Netflix movie was on, so...tomorrow you'll be totally healthy! But you can get a handle on taking care of yourself. Let's do this!

What a Workout!

Setting your **fitness goals** isn't just about deciding to hit the gym or jog around the block; it's about crafting **a plan that fits you** like your favorite pair of sneakers—comfortable yet effective. First up, let's talk about tailoring these goals. You won't train like a marathon runner if you hate running, right? Instead, focus on activities that light a spark in you. Love dancing? Consider classes that infuse cardio through dance. Prefer tranquility? Maybe yoga or Pilates is your thing. The key is to align your fitness routine with **what makes you feel good,** physically and mentally. This approach ensures you stick with it because it doesn't feel like a chore.

When setting these goals, **realism** is your best friend. Aiming to bench press 300 pounds on your first day at the gym is like trying to climb Everest in flip-flops—ambitious but not exactly practical. **Start small.** Maybe it's doing ten push-ups a day or jogging twice a week. As these tasks become less daunting, ramp up the intensity or frequency. Remember, fitness is a personal journey (not a sprint), and the goals should evolve as you grow stronger and more confident.

Now, onto **building a balanced routine.** Think of your workout schedule as a well-rounded diet. Just like you wouldn't eat only apples for every meal, you shouldn't just run daily. **Mix it up** with various exercises targeting different areas of fitness: cardiovascular for heart health, strength training for muscle building, flexibility exercises for agility, and balance workouts to keep you steady on your feet. This **variety** keeps your routine interesting and allows different muscle groups to work and recover, reducing the risk of injury.

Cardio could be anything that gets your heart rate up—jump rope, cycling, or brisk walking. Strength training might involve weights or body-weight exercises like squats and sit-ups. Yoga or a simple stretch routine at the end of your workout can do wonders for flexibility. Lastly, incorporate **balance exercises** like tai chi or stand on one leg exercises that you can even do while brushing your teeth. This holistic approach ensures you're working out and crafting a stronger, more versatile body.

Combatting **the common barriers** to exercise is crucial. "I don't have time" is probably the biggest wall to climb. But here's the thing: workouts don't need to be hour-long ordeals. Science says even **short bursts of exercise**, like 15-20 minutes, can significantly boost your health if done regularly. Maybe a quick jog before breakfast or a workout video between homework sessions. **Find pockets of time** that work for you and guard them fiercely.

Motivation can also be a slippery fish. One day you're pumped, ready to conquer the world. Next, even lifting the remote feels like a workout. To stay motivated, **set clear, achievable milestones and reward yourself** when you hit them. Did you stick to your workout schedule all week? Treat yourself to a movie night. Reached a new fitness milestone? Grab that new book you've been eyeing. These **little rewards** keep the dopamine flowing and your motivation tank full.

Tracking your progress is not just about patting yourself on the back; it's about recalibrating as you evolve. Use apps or a good old-fashioned journal to **keep tabs on what you're doing and how it's making you feel**. Maybe you'll notice that jogging isn't your jam, but swimming makes you feel like a superhero. Listening to your body is key. It tells you when to push harder or take a step back. This feedback loop lets you adjust your goals and methods, making your routine enjoyable. So lace up your sneakers, and let's make fitness fun and fulfilling, one step at a time.

Smell the Roses

Stress is like that annoying classmate who just won't let you focus. It's **that existential dread** that creeps up on you and messes with your head; if you don't deal with it, it can seriously cramp your style. Recognizing the signs of **stress** is crucial, not just for acing your next test, but for maintaining your overall chill vibe. So, **what does stress look like?** It's not just biting your nails during finals week. It can be that constant feeling of exhaustion no matter how much you sleep or that irritable mood that turns you into a walking eye roll. It can mess with your stomach, make your heart race, and make it hard to concentrate on your favorite show.

The trick is **catching these signs early.** Just like knowing when your phone needs a charge before it dies during your favorite influencer's live stream, recognizing stress signals helps you manage them before they take over. Keep a mood diary or use an app to track your daily feelings. You might start to **see patterns**— maybe you're more stressed on Mondays because you're worried about the pile of homework from the weekend. Knowing **what triggers your stress** is half the battle.

Now, how about some killer moves to knock out stress? Let's start with **deep breathing** exercises. It sounds too simple to be effective, but just like rebooting your computer can magically fix issues, resetting your breath can work wonders. **Try the 4-7-8 technique**: breathe in for four seconds, hold it for seven, and exhale slowly for eight. It's a mini-vacation for your brain and body. **Yoga and meditation** are also fantastic stress-busters. They're like the quiet eye of your daily hurricane, allowing you to stretch, chill, and regroup. **Even a few minutes can make a difference.** Roll out a mat, strike a pose, and find your inner Zen. YouTube and apps like Headspace or Calm offer guided sessions that can make yoga and meditation feel like hanging out with a laid-back friend who wants you to feel good.

Balancing school, life, and everything else can make you wish for a 28-hour day, but since time travel isn't an option, let's talk about **time management**. It's being the DJ of your own life, mixing your tracks to keep the vibe upbeat without letting any one tune take over. Create a schedule that's realistic, not one that assumes you'll turn into a superhero who doesn't need downtime. **Use tools** like Google Calendar or Trello to keep track of assignments, practices, and social commitments. And here's a radical idea: **schedule breaks**. Yes, actually, put *"do nothing"* on your calendar. These breaks are your brain's snack time—they help you digest information and come back to your tasks refreshed.

But what if stress gets too real and your usual tricks aren't cutting it? This is when you lean on others. **Reach out to friends, family, or a counselor.** You're not dumping your problems on them; you're sharing what's on your mind and finding solutions together. Sometimes, **just talking** about what's stressing you out can lighten the load and make it easier to handle. Schools often have **resources like counselors** who are there to help—you're not alone, even though it might feel like it sometimes.

Lastly, **pick five things** you're grateful for when you wake up in the morning and again at night. Training your mind to be in **gratitude** mode is the secret sauce to keeping that relaxed vibe going. Do you have a bed to sleep in, clothes to wear, and something good to eat for breakfast? Appreciating even the little things that make your life wonderful is the best medicine.

Please See a Doctor About That

Navigating the **healthcare system** can sometimes feel like you're trying to solve a Rubik's cube—blindfolded. But hey, just like any puzzle, it's not so daunting once you know a few tricks. Let's start with finding **the right doctor.** Think of it like casting for the lead role in your personal health saga—you want a star performer who gets rave reviews and understands your script. Start by checking out their credentials and specialties. Are they **board-certified** in their field? That's like having a top-tier badge in a video game, representing a high level of expertise.

Next up, consider their **communication style.** You want someone who doesn't just talk medical jargon but actually speaks your language. During your first visit, see if they listen well, explain things clearly, and seem **genuinely interested in your well-being.** It's like a first date—except instead of sharing a coffee, you're sharing your health concerns. Also, location and availability are key. A great doctor who's always overbooked or located hours away might not be the best fit if you need care that fits into your hectic teen life. Check out online reviews and ask for recommendations from friends or family.

Now, let's decode the beast that is **health insurance.** If insurance policies were a textbook, they'd be the kind that's thick enough to double as a personal defense weapon. But don't worry, it's not as complex as it seems. Start with the basics: premiums, deductibles, copays, and coverage. Think of **premiums** like a subscription fee you pay for your insurance plan. You pay the **deductible** out of pocket before your insurance starts sharing the costs. It's like the initial amount you must cover in a game before unlocking the next level.

How do you get **insurance coverage?** In the United States today, unless you work for a very small company, your employer usually provides health insurance if you work full-time. Children are generally allowed to stay on their parent's health insurance until age 26, though a few states allow it until age 30. Health insurance is required in some states, or you'll be fined at tax time. Yep, it's rough out there. **Check your state's guidelines.** Not on your parent's health insurance? Time to get your own full-time job and **employer-sponsored health coverage**, which is still the best deal around. Or you can **buy your own policy** online, but remember that this will make a several hundred-dollar dent in your monthly budget and far, far fewer tacos for Tuesdays.

Copays are the fixed amounts you pay for certain services, like a doctor's visit or filling a prescription. Finally, **coverage** details what services and treatments are included. Some plans cover things like mental health services and physical therapy, while others might not. Make sure you understand what's covered so you're not surprised later.

Got a highly **personal medical concern** that needs attention? **Privacy and confidentiality** are huge in healthcare. Just because you're not legally an adult doesn't mean you don't have rights. **Confidentiality** means that what you discuss with your doctor stays private, not shared with anyone—not even your parents—without your permission. This is super important, especially when dealing with sensitive issues. **Be completely honest** with your healthcare provider. If you're not upfront about what's bothering you, they can't give you the care you need.

Understanding how to navigate these aspects of healthcare **empowers you** to make health decisions confidently. So, step up, take control, and remember: Your health is worth every bit of effort you put into understanding these essentials.

Sleep Science: Why It Matters

Let's talk about **sleep**, that magical realm where you're the star of your own bizarre, often forgotten movies. But beyond being the best free entertainment your brain provides, sleep is like the ultimate Swiss army knife for your health. **It boosts everything from your brainpower and mood to your physical well-being.** Ever noticed how everything feels like an uphill battle after a bad night's sleep? That's because sleep isn't just downtime; it's when your body and mind go into overdrive, repairing, rejuvenating, and recharging. It's hitting the **reset button** - or better yet, turning it off and on again, ensuring everything runs smoothly.

Now, this nightly reboot affects your mood and cognitive abilities in ways that make caffeine jealous. A solid night's sleep can enhance your **memory, creativity, and problem-solving skills**, making you more effective at acing tests and mastering new dance moves. It also **regulates the hormones** that affect your mood, helping to keep those inexplicable bouts of teen angst in check. But when you skimp on sleep, it's not just your energy that crashes; your brain functions get foggy, and your **emotions** can swing like a pendulum on overdrive.

So, how do you lock down a sleep routine that would make even Sleeping Beauty envious? It starts with **consistency**. Try to hit the hay and wake up at the same time every day (yes, even on weekends!). This helps set **your body's internal clock**, making it easier to fall asleep and wake up naturally - no alarm clock required. (This actually works - I get up at the same time every day, and I haven't needed to use an alarm clock in years!). Create a pre-sleep ritual that helps you wind down. This could be as simple as reading a book (sorry, textbooks don't count), listening to calming music, or doing gentle stretches. The goal is to signal your brain that it's time to slow down and prepare for shutdown.

But what about those nights when sleep plays hard to get? You're tossing and turning, counting more sheep than a shepherd, and sleep remains a distant dream. Common issues like **insomnia or delayed sleep phase syndrome**, where your sleep pattern is delayed by two or more hours beyond the socially acceptable bedtime, can turn your night into a frustrating vigil. If these restless nights become the norm rather than the exception, it might be time to **seek help.** Start with your family doctor, who can guide you to a sleep specialist if necessary. Sometimes, just understanding that your sleep issues are not uncommon can ease your mind, and solutions like maintaining a sleep diary or practicing cognitive-behavioral techniques can be effective tools to conquer the night.

In today's digital age, another **sleep thief** often goes unchecked: your beloved screens. Whether it's a late-night Netflix binge, scrolling through social media, or texting into the wee hours, **screen time before bed is like a double espresso for your brain.** The blue light emitted by screens inhibits melatonin production, the hormone that tells your body it is time to sleep. So, what's a tech-savvy teen to do? **Power down all electronic devices *at least an hour before bed*.** If you must use your devices, switch on a blue light filter, available on most smartphones, tablets, and computers, reducing blue light exposure. Also, consider the type of content you're consuming. Swap out high-energy video games or edge-of-your-seat shows for something more calming, like a podcast or an eBook with a black background to minimize light exposure.

Navigating the world of sleep is crucial, not just for your physical and mental health but for your overall quality of life. By understanding **the importance of sleep, establishing a consistent routine,** addressing sleep issues proactively, and managing your screen time, you're setting the stage for better sleep and brighter days. So tonight, as you lay your head down, remember that every hour of good sleep is a step towards a healthier, happier you. Sweet dreams, and may your sleep be as rejuvenating as a weekend spent chilling with friends.

Mental Health Signs, Resources, and Stigma

Navigating the maze of mental health isn't like following a recipe where you can just mix up a few ingredients and expect a perfect outcome. It's more like being a detective in your own psychological thriller, where understanding clues, patterns, and behaviors can either plot a path to wellness or leave you running in circles. Recognizing the early signs of common mental health issues such as **anxiety, depression, and eating disorders is crucial**. These signs are **red flags** waving in your mental landscape. Maybe you're feeling more than just blue for days on end, finding little joy in activities you once loved, or perhaps food and weight concerns are starting to dominate your thoughts. These signals are your mind's way of saying, "Hey, we need to talk."

It's not just about spotting these signs in yourself; it's also about observing them in friends. You know how you can tell when your friend is upset even when they insist they're "fine"? It's like that, but deeper. If you notice **a friend withdrawing** from social activities, drastically changing their eating habits, or expressing overwhelming feelings of guilt or worthlessness, these are cues that they're battling something internally. Opening up a supportive conversation can be a game-changer. You may not be able to solve their problems—but you need to let them know you're there and that they're not navigating this tough terrain alone.

Now, let's talk about resources because understanding the problem is only half the battle; knowing where to turn for help is key. Picture this as **your toolbox**—filled not with wrenches and screwdrivers but with hotlines, websites, and community services.

Places like the **National Alliance on Mental Illness (NAMI)** or the **Crisis Text Line** offer immediate, free support and guidance. Schools often have counselors trained to deal with these very issues, and no, visiting them doesn't mean you're "crazy" or "weak." It means you're smart enough to know when to seek reinforcements. There are also **apps designed to help manage anxiety and mood**, offering a tech-savvy approach to traditional mental health strategies.

But here's the kicker: even with all these tools at our disposal, the stigma surrounding mental health can make it as challenging to talk about as explaining why you're a fan of the most hated band in school. **Breaking this stigma** starts with a **conversation**—open, honest, and judgment-free. It's **changing the narrative** from "mental health issues are for the weak" to "it's okay not to be okay." Schools, social media, and even at home are all battlegrounds where stigma can be reinforced or dismantled. By sharing stories, whether it's through campaigns, classes, or casual chats, we chip away at the **misconceptions surrounding mental health**, paving the way for a more understanding and supportive environment.

Self-care is the main ingredient in the recipe for **mental well-being**. It's not all spa days and bubble baths (though those are nice); it's also about setting boundaries, knowing when to take a break from social media, and engaging in activities that recharge your mental batteries. Whether journaling to sort through your thoughts, hitting the gym to shed some stress, or simply carving out time to read your favorite book, these acts of self-care are not selfish—they're **essential maintenance for your mental health.** Mental health is not a destination but a continuous journey, and with the right tools and support, it's one that you can navigate successfully.

EIGHT

Is This Legal?

> *Dance like nobody's watching; email like it may one day*
> *be read aloud in a deposition.*
>
> Anonymous

Have you ever felt like you were playing a game of Monopoly, but instead of fake money and property, the stakes involved real-world rights and laws? Welcome to the grown-up table, where understanding **your legal rights** is about more than avoiding jail time with a Get Out of Jail Free card. It's knowing how to navigate the complex world of legalities that suddenly apply to you now that you're stepping into adult sneakers. So, buckle up! We're about to take a whirlwind tour of your legal rights in school, work, and those awkward moments when you might bump into law enforcement.

You Have the Right!

First, let's talk about **your rights at school and work**—because, yes, even as a teen, you have rights in these battlegrounds. In school, **your rights include** freedom of speech, some privacy rights (like your locker), and the right to a free education without discrimination. This means you can wear that funky hat that screams your political or religious beliefs as long as it doesn't **disrupt the peace**. And about those surprise locker checks? Generally, schools need a reasonable suspicion to rummage through your personal space. It's like they need a mini-warrant from the principal's office.

Now, shifting to **your job**—if you're juggling work with school, kudos to you! You're entitled to **fair treatment** here too. This includes earning **at least the minimum wage** and working in a **safe environment**. Got a boss who thinks safety goggles are for nerds? Nope, not okay. And if you're thinking about blowing the whistle on safety issues, federal and state laws have your back to protect you from retaliation. You have a legal shield in case things get dicey.

Encountering a police officer can be nerve-wracking, but it's less scary when you know your rights. If you're stopped, stay calm, be polite, and remember: **you have the right to remain silent**. Really, you can keep those lips zipped until you've got a lawyer, even if you're just being questioned. If you're on the move and an officer stops you, **ask if you're free to go**. If they say yes, walk away calmly. If they say no, you're being detained, but remember, **staying silent** until you have legal representation is **your golden ticket**.

Privacy might seem like an old-school concept in the age of social media oversharing. However, laws like **COPPA** (Children's Online

Privacy Protection Act) and **FERPA** (Family Educational Rights and Privacy Act) are here to **protect your personal information both online and at school**. COPPA protects your online info from prying commercial interests, ensuring websites get parental consent before collecting data from kids under 13. Meanwhile, FERPA shields your school records. So, no, the school can't just give your grades out like free movie tickets without your permission.

Turning 18 might feel like unlocking a new level in the game of life, but it also comes with new legal responsibilities and rights. **This age of majority** means you can now **vote**, make contracts in your name (hello, credit cards, and car loans), and even sue or be sued. But what if you're under 18 and ready to be your own boss, legally speaking? That's where **emancipation** comes into play. If you're thinking about this **legal independence**, you'll need to prove you can handle your own affairs, which includes managing finances and making mature decisions. Think of it as a legal declaration that you're playing the game of life on hard mode.

Navigating the maze of legal rights and responsibilities might seem daunting, but arming yourself with this knowledge is like having a cheat code for adulthood. Each piece of knowledge empowers you to handle real-life challenges with confidence. So, keep these insights in your back pocket, ready to pull out like a superhero's trusty tool whenever you face a legal conundrum.

Surfing the Legal System

So, you've found yourself in a bit of a pickle, and now you're staring down the barrel of the legal system. First things first, let's talk about getting some backup in the form of **legal representation**. Whether you're dealing with minor infractions or more serious allegations, having a sharp legal mind in your corner can make all the difference. But where do you find these legal wizards? Start with **referrals from family or friends**, or sift through online directories. Most attorneys offer initial consultations **free of charge**, so you can get the vibe check done without spending a dime.

If the cash flow situation resembles a dried-up creek, **public defenders** are your go-to. These are **court-appointed attorneys** for those who can't afford private counsel, and while they often get a bad rap for being overworked, many are passionate about justice and highly capable. If you qualify for a public defender, remember they are there to serve **your best interests. Communicate openly with them**, provide all the necessary information they might need to defend you, and do not be shy about asking questions. You have the right to understand every part of your defense, no matter who represents you.

Diving into the **juvenile justice process** is a bit like a Choose Your Own Adventure book, but the stakes are real, and the outcomes can seriously affect your future. When minors are accused of crimes, the cases usually go through **juvenile court**, which focuses more on **rehabilitation** than punishment. This system recognizes that kids can make poor choices but also have the potential to learn and grow from their mistakes. However, depending on the severity of the crime, juveniles can sometimes be **tried as adults**, leading to harsher sentences. Knowing the ins and outs of this process is crucial. It **empowers you to navigate** the proceedings and possibly **advocate** for alternative resolutions like community service or counseling, which could steer you away from harsher penalties.

Understanding your rights during these proceedings is like having a cheat sheet during an exam. Always remember: **you have the right to remain silent**, and anything you say can indeed be used against you. You also have **the right to an attorney**; if you can't afford one, the court will provide a public defender. Beyond these, you're entitled to **a fair and speedy trial** and have **the right to confront any witnesses who testify against you**. If things don't go your way, you also have **the right to appeal the decision**. These rights are your armor; knowing them can help you defend yourself effectively in the legal arena.

Finally, let's touch on something many teens worry about—**the long-term impact of having a juvenile record**. Having a record can be like walking around with a heavy backpack full of bricks; it can affect your job prospects, college applications, and more. But here's a glimmer of hope—**expungement**. This is the legal equivalent of a giant eraser that **can wipe your slate clean**. Each state has rules about which offenses can be expunged and the process involved, but typically, you must show that you've stayed out of trouble for a certain period and have rehabilitated. Securing an expungement can lift that weight off your shoulders, making your missteps as a youth less of a burden as you stride into adulthood.

Navigating the legal system might feel overwhelming like you're trying to solve a Rubik's cube blindfolded. But with the right knowledge and support, you can tackle it head-on. Every step you take is a learning opportunity and a chance to **advocate for yourself**. Keep your head up, stay informed, and take control of your story.

Rights in the Workplace

Navigating your first job or any part-time gig while **juggling the demands** of high school and your social life is like trying to fit your entire sock collection into one drawer—something's gotta give! You've got to be a time management ninja and know your rights at work. Yup, even part-timers and job newbies have protections. You're not just last season's tech—easily replaced and forgotten. Remember, **you've got rights**, so don't let anyone treat you like an old flip phone!

First up, let's chat about the **minimum wage**. This isn't just the lowest amount you can be paid to afford those concert tickets—it's **a legally protected baseline that employers can't dip below**. Whether you're flipping burgers, stacking shelves, or coding websites, **knowing the minimum wage in your area is crucial**. If your paycheck seems a bit light, it might be time to do some digging and see if your employer is playing by the rules. Remember, **every state can set its own minimum wage, and sometimes, local areas like cities or counties might nudge that number up a bit**. So, doing your homework could literally pay off.

Now, let's talk about **work hours and conditions**. Something called the Fair Labor Standards Act (FLSA) sounds about as exciting as watching paint dry but stick with me—it's pretty important. It sets the standards for work hours, overtime pay, and the **conditions** under which you can work. For instance, if you're under 18, there are **clear rules** about how many hours you can work during the school week, which jobs are off-limits due to safety concerns, and what times of day you can legally work. It's like having a legal curfew that ensures you're not overworked and under-rested.

But what if your workplace feels more like a scene from a survival reality show than a professional environment? That's where **safety regulations** come in. The Occupational Safety and Health Administration **(OSHA)** is the big player here, ensuring your workplace doesn't double as a hazard zone. This means everything from **proper training on equipment** to the availability of **safety gear** should be a given, not a perk. If things seem unsafe, speaking up is your right. It's not just about avoiding a trip to the ER—it's about ensuring everyone, including the next wave of workers, has a safe place to earn their keep.

Discrimination and harassment are ugly beasts in any scenario, but in the workplace, they're especially loathsome. You have **the right to work without being harassed or discriminated against because of your race, color, religion, sex, national origin, disability, or age.** This includes unwanted comments, jokes, or advances and extends to hiring, firing, promotions, and job assignments. It's a shield; use it if needed. If you ever feel targeted, most workplaces have a process for **reporting these issues**—usually starting with your HR department. It's crucial to document everything and seek support early for your sake and to ensure the cycle doesn't continue with others.

Lastly, let's dive into the somewhat murky waters of workers' compensation and employment contracts. **Workers' compensation** is like a financial first aid kit. If you get injured on the job, this system covers **medical costs and lost wages** while you recover. It's not dependent on proving your employer was at fault—instead, it operates under a no-fault system where the key is that **the injury happened on the job**. Understanding this can differentiate between a stressful recovery and a supported one. As for **employment contracts**, they might seem straightforward, but the devil is often in the details. Always **read these documents** thoroughly before signing. Legal jargon might be worth getting some guidance if it isn't your thing. Think of it as translating a foreign language— one slip could mean agreeing to conditions you didn't intend, like mandatory overtime or waived rights.

Navigating your rights in the workplace is about empowerment. Knowing these rights helps protect you and sets a standard for how you expect to be treated and what you're willing to accept. So, stay informed, stay vigilant, and remember, even as a young employee, **you're entitled to a legal and ethical workplace that respects and values your contributions**.

Civic Engagement: Democracy!

So, you're a freshly minted adult, and it's time to toss your hat into the ring of democracy. First order of business? **Registering to vote**. You're signing up for the national club where every member has the power to shape the future. This is your VIP pass to the party of civic responsibility. Registering is easy. Just hit up your state or local election office website, or check out online portals like **Vote.gov.** Fill out some basic info, and boom, you're ready to rock the vote. You can vote in most states by mail, no standing in long lines shivering in the rain. Remember, voting isn't just a right; it's **a rite of passage** into the world of adulting where **your voice** can actually dictate the plot twists in the real-world saga of our nation.

But why stop at voting? **Civic engagement** has more layers than your favorite triple-decker burger. You can **volunteer for political campaigns**, where you get a backstage pass to the gritty, not-always-glamorous world of getting someone elected. Hand out flyers, make calls, or help manage social media campaigns—all while soaking up the electric atmosphere of political strategizing. This is more than wearing a candidate's pin; it's about being part of a movement and **finding your tribe** in the chaos of political discourse.

And hey, engagement doesn't end with politics. Dive into **community service**. Whether cleaning up parks, tutoring kids, or dishing out meals at a local shelter, community service isn't just good for college apps—it's **good for the soul**. It connects you to your community on a visceral level, showing you the direct impact of your efforts. You can see your actions ripple outward, **improving**

lives in tangible ways. That's the kind of real-life karma that no amount of online likes can buy.

Understanding **the cogs and gears of government** isn't just for poli-sci majors. Grasping how laws are made, how policies are formed, and **how government structures affect your daily life** can turn you from a passive observer into an active participant. Knowing the rules of a game makes playing it more effective and a lot more fun. This understanding empowers you to **advocate for changes that matter**. Want cleaner streets, better schools, or more parks? Knowing whom to talk to and how to talk to them can turn your ideas into action. Learn how to **make the system work for you** instead of feeling worked over by the system.

So, get out there. Register to vote. Volunteer. Dive into community service. Decode the mechanisms of government. These aren't just civic duties; they're opportunities to wield influence, to be the change-maker. **You have the power to sculpt the future**, to leave your mark on the world in indelible ink. Don't just stand by and watch history unfold—grab a pen and write some of it yourself. Because when it comes to democracy, the more you put in, the more we all get out. And that's a win not just for you but for everyone.

NINE

Keep Calm and Carry On

S o, you've just been handed the keys to **your first car**. Exciting, right? But before you peel out of the driveway, dreaming of open roads and new adventures, car maintenance is a tiny detail worth considering. Yes, it sounds about as thrilling as watching paint dry, but hear me out. Knowing the basics of car care is like having a superpower. It keeps your ride smooth, your wallet happy, and you far away from the side of the road, looking bewildered with a smoking engine.

Basic Car Maintenance

First things first, let's talk about **buying a car**. Whether it's a shiny new model or a trusty old set of wheels, the key is to **choose a car that fits your budget and needs**, not just your style. Think about fuel efficiency, reliability, and maintenance costs. A sports car might look cool, but it might not be the smartest choice if it guzzles gas like you guzzle soda. And don't forget about **insurance. Shop around for rates**, and remember, your dream car might be everyone else's, too—which could drive up insurance costs.

Now, onto **the emergency kit**. This isn't your typical school backpack. This kit should contain **essentials** like first aid supplies, jumper cables, tire-changing equipment, flashlights, and batteries. Think of it as your "Oh no!" kit. Flat tire? No problem. Dead battery? You've got it covered. You'll be the hero of your road trip, ready to tackle whatever potholes life throws. **Consider joining AAA**. When your car dies on the side of the road in the middle of nowhere, AAA has your back, coming with a tow truck if necessary to replace a tire or dead battery. AAA also provides insurance and car purchasing assistance. **It's a great deal.**

Next up is the nitty-gritty of **car maintenance**. Checking your oil regularly is like checking your phone battery—it tells you how much 'life' your car has left before needing a recharge. If your dashboard doesn't electronically alert you when your oil gets low, you must get under the hood. Pull out the dipstick, wipe it clean, dip it back in, and check the level and color. Dark or dirty oil needs a change, and generally, you should **change your oil** every 5,000 miles or so, but check your owner's manual to be sure. While you're at it, peek at **your air filter, transmission fluid, and coolant levels.** These are the lifeblood of your car, and keeping them clean and full can prevent automotive anemia.

Don't forget your **tires and windshield wipers**. Tires should be rotated every 5,000 to 7,000 miles to wear evenly, extending their life and giving you better traction. Ever heard of **the penny tire test**? Stick a penny head-first into the tread. If you can see all of Lincoln's head, it's time for new tires. As for **wipers**, if they leave streaks or gaps, replace them. It's like swapping out a bad marker during a whiteboard presentation—clarity is key.

Regular tune-ups are your car's spa days. They keep everything running smoothly, catching potential issues before they turn into wallet-gobbling monsters. And about those strange noises—**don't ignore them**. A squeal when you brake, or a clunk when you turn can be signs of trouble. Your car is trying to tell you something. Listen to it.

Handling a **dead battery or an overheated engine** can seem daunting. If your car's battery dies, a good set of jumper cables and a friendly driver can have you back on the road in minutes. Overheating? Pull over, turn off the engine, and let it cool. Keep an eye on the temperature gauge, and if this becomes a regular thing, **see a mechanic**. It could be a simple fix, like topping off the coolant or something more serious.

Car maintenance might not be glamorous, but **it's essential**. Like brushing your teeth or combing your hair, it's part of the routine that keeps you looking good, feeling good, and ready to roll. So, grab that owner's manual, roll up your sleeves, and get ready to dive under the hood. Your car and your future self will thank you.

Does Anyone Know CPR?

Let's dive into something you might equate with dramatic TV hospital scenes but is indeed a critical skill set you'd want in your back pocket—**handling emergencies like a pro**. Imagine you're at a barbecue, and someone starts choking on a hot dog, or during a casual soccer game, a friend collapses. Not exactly your typical day, right? Knowing CPR and the Heimlich maneuver can literally make the difference between life and death. So, let's break it down.

CPR, or Cardio-Pulmonary Resuscitation, sounds like a fancy dance move but trust me, it's one you'll want to master. This technique is **crucial when someone's breathing or heartbeat has stopped. Here's how you do it:** first, ensure the scene is safe. Next, lay the person on their back and kneel beside their chest. Place the heel of one hand on the center of their chest, put your other hand on top, and interlock your fingers. Keep your arms straight, and use your body weight to press down hard and fast. Your aim is 100-120 compressions per minute—think of the beat of a fast-paced song like "Stayin' Alive" by the Bee Gees (yes, the irony). If you've been trained, you can alternate compressions with rescue breaths, but if not, **hands-only** CPR is still highly effective.

Now onto **the Heimlich maneuver—your go-to move when someone is choking. Stand behind the person,** wrap your arms around their waist, and make a fist with one hand. Place it just above their belly button, grab the fist with your other hand, and give a quick, upward thrust. **Repeat** this until the blockage is dislodged. Remember, it's like trying to lift them off the ground slightly with each thrust—not too gently, but you're not trying to launch them into space either.

Moving on to something a bit less intense but equally important— **treating wounds and burns.** Let's say you're cooking and accidentally grab a hot pan, or you scrape your knee falling off a skateboard. First, **clean the wound.** Run it under cool water works, and gently clean around the wound with soap. Avoid getting soap directly in it, though—it's not a bubble bath. For minor burns, keep it under **cool** (not cold) water for about 10-20 minutes. Then,

cover it with a sterile, non-fluffy cloth or dressing to protect it from infection. Watch for **signs of infection** like increased redness, swelling, or pus. If you see these, or if the wound is deep (like you can see bone—yikes!), it's doctor time.

Next up, **anaphylaxis**—this isn't just a regular allergy. It's **severe and can escalate quickly**, making it crucial to recognize and **act fast. Symptoms** might include a rash, swelling, difficulty breathing, or a sudden feeling of doom (and not just because you forgot to study for a test). If someone has **a known severe allergy**, they likely carry an epinephrine auto-injector, commonly known as an EpiPen. You might have to step in if they're too overwhelmed to use it. Hold the **EpiPen** with the orange tip pointing downward, remove the cap, and jab it firmly into their outer thigh. Hold it there for about 3 seconds (count slowly). **Then, call emergency services** because they will need to check that everything else is okay.

Lastly, know **when to call for help** because sometimes, **being a hero means dialing 911.** If you are ever unsure about a situation— if an injury seems worse than a minor cut, if someone's condition rapidly declines, or if an allergic reaction includes trouble breathing—**always err on the side of caution and call the pros.** It's better to have help you don't end up needing than to need help you didn't call for.

Mastering these skills might seem daunting, but they equip you to handle life's curveballs, whether they're thrown at you or someone near you. So take a deep breath, and maybe even sign up for a first aid course if you're feeling really pumped. You've got this—ready to handle burns from a rogue BBQ or save the day in a more serious pinch.

Supporting Peers in Crisis

Imagine you're at a party, and amidst the laughter and music, you notice a friend sitting quietly in the corner, looking more like they're at a funeral than a Friday night hangout. Something seems off. This is where your mental health first aid skills kick in, superhero style. It's not about swooping in with dramatic gestures but about recognizing signs that **a friend might be struggling** and knowing how to approach them with care and sensitivity.

As mentioned earlier, the first step is learning to **spot those signs of crisis**. It's not always about the obvious things like crying or freaking out. Sometimes, it's in **the quieter signals**—maybe they're withdrawing from the group, showing a lack of interest in things they used to love, or making offhand remarks about self-harm. **These are your cues** that something deeper might be going on. Be the person who picks up on subtle hints that others might miss. Recognizing these signs early can be crucial in providing timely support.

Once you've noticed these signs, the next step is to **engage through active listening**. This isn't just about nodding and throwing in an occasional "uh-huh." It's about really hearing them. **Create a space where they feel safe** to open up, free from judgment or interruptions. Use open body language and make eye contact to show you're fully present. Ask gentle, **open-ended questions** that encourage them to express themselves. Phrases like "It seems like you've been having a hard time, want to talk about it?" can open the door for them to share their feelings. Remember, this is not the time for advice or fixing their problems—it's about **letting them know they're not alone and you're there to listen.**

However, there will be times when listening isn't enough, and **professional help is needed**. This can be tricky, especially if your friend is hesitant or defensive about seeking help. It's important to **approach this sensitively** without making them feel pressured. Suggesting professional help should be done with care, emphasizing that it's not because you think they're broken, but because you believe they deserve the best support possible. You could say something like, "I really think it might help to talk to someone who can provide more support than I can. Maybe we can look at some options together?" You're **being supportive, not directive**. Offer to help them find a counselor or therapist, or if they're not ready to take that step, help them reach out to trusted adults who can guide them.

Supporting a friend in crisis can be **emotionally taxing**, so it is vital to **look after your own mental health as well**. This is where setting **boundaries** comes into play. It's okay to admit when things are beyond your ability to help. You're a friend, not a therapist. Make sure to engage in activities that replenish your own emotional well-being. Whether hanging out with other friends, engaging in hobbies, or just taking time for yourself, **keeping your emotional batteries charged is imperative.** It ensures that you can be there for your friend without burning out. Remember, you can't pour from an empty cup.

Navigating the challenges of helping a friend through a mental health crisis **requires compassion, patience, and resilience.** By learning to recognize the signs of crisis, engaging in active listening, encouraging professional help, and maintaining your own mental health, you equip yourself to be a supportive and empowering presence for those in need.

Everybody Stay Calm

When it comes to emergencies, most of us would rather think about literally anything else. Wouldn't you rather binge-watch a series than prepare for **a power outage** or—dare we say—**a natural disaster?** But being prepped isn't just for the "doomsday ready" crowd; it's for anyone who likes being able to handle whatever life throws their way. So, let's roll up our sleeves and dive into the nitty-gritty of staying safe, starting with your emergency kit.

Think of your **emergency kit** like your essential festival pack—**items you need for survival** but tailored for actual survival. Not glow sticks and cool hats, but **water, non-perishable snacks, a flashlight, extra batteries, a first aid kit, and perhaps the most forgotten hero—cash.** Yep, good old-fashioned paper money because not everywhere can take cards during a power outage. And don't forget **personal items** like extra glasses or medications. Store these goodies in a couple of waterproof bins or backpacks, which are easy to grab if you need to evacuate or move to a safer location in your home. You're packing for a spontaneous adventure; only this one can save your life.

Now, onto crafting **your emergency plan.** This is not a school fire drill; it's the real deal. Start by finding **some safe spots** where your family can meet up—one outside your home and another outside your neighborhood. Why two? Because you never know what the situation will be. There may be a gas leak at home, or the entire area is affected. Next, **list your emergency contacts**, including a friend or relative who lives out of town. Why someone out of town? Because local lines might be jammed during a major disaster, and Aunt Sharon in the next state could be your lifeline to coordinating family whereabouts.

Moving into **fire safety,** let's light up some knowledge without sparking flames. First on the list are **smoke detectors** - your fire alarm before you even smell the smoke. Ensure you have one in every bedroom, outside sleeping areas, and every level of your home, including the basement. **Test them monthly,** and change the batteries at least once a year—maybe at the same time you update your clocks for daylight saving time. It's a simple step that can have a considerable impact.

Next up, **fire extinguishers.** Having one in your kitchen (away from the stove), near your fireplace if you have one, and in the garage can make a big difference. But it isn't enough to have them; you need to **know how to use them. Remember the acronym PASS:** Pull the pin, aim low at the base of the fire, Squeeze the trigger slowly, and sweep the nozzle from side to side. Practice this motion when you check the extinguisher's pressure, which should be part of your regular home maintenance check-up

Here's another pro tip: get an **emergency fire blanket** or several. I got mine on Amazon. This handy item can extinguish fire immediately without having to wrestle with fire extinguisher nozzles. Store it where you can grab it quickly. Have both items on hand just to be safe.

On to the **first aid basics.** While you might think first aid is just bandaging up a scraped knee, it's your frontline defense in a medical emergency. **Building a basic first aid kit** is straightforward: bandages in various sizes, gauze, adhesive tape, scissors, tweezers, antiseptic wipes, and a cold compress. Let's not forget over-the-counter pain relievers, allergy meds, and hydrocortisone cream. Keep these in your emergency kit, and maybe have a smaller version in your car or backpack. **Know how to use them,** too—like knowing pressure points to stop bleeding or how to clean a wound can prevent a bad situation from worsening.

Lastly, let's touch on **some basic survival skills**. Knowing how to **shut off your home's water, gas, and electricity** can prevent further hazards like flooding or fire after an earthquake or severe storm. Keep tools handy near these shut-off valves and ensure everyone in the house knows how to use them. If you're in an area prone to natural disasters like hurricanes or tornadoes, reinforcing your knowledge of **local emergency plans and evacuation routes** is necessary. And for those adventurous souls who might find themselves **lost in the woods,** understanding basic navigation skills, **how to signal for help**, and basic shelter-building techniques can turn you into a real-life action hero. Breathe and stay calm under pressure.

Keep Your Balance

Maybe you are juggling three flaming torches: schoolwork, work, and oh-so-precious personal time. Mastering the art of **prioritization** is about keeping those torches in the air without setting anything (like your hair) on fire. Let's kick off by explaining how to **sort through your responsibilities.** Picture your tasks as a bunch of apps running on your phone. Some are power-hungry games that drain your battery (like that group project due next week), while others are more like your basic clock app—useful but not urgent. The trick is identifying which tasks need immediate energy and which can run in the background for a bit longer.

Start by making a list—yes, the old-school way. Write down everything you need to do, from homework to chores, and then rank these tasks by urgency and importance. Anything with a deadline looming or carries enormous consequences if delayed (think term papers, not vacuuming your room) gets top billing. This process clears your mind and puts **a game plan** right in front of your eyes. And speaking of plans, let's discuss **integrating practical tools** that keep you on track.

In this digital age, your smartphone is your best ally. **Use calendar apps** to set reminders for important dates. Plug in everything from exam dates to shifts at the part-time gig. The beauty of these apps? They nag you so your mom doesn't have to. **Apps like Trello or Asana** can help manage more significant projects **by breaking them down into bite-sized tasks**. Each task gets a 'card' that you can move from 'To Do' to 'Doing' to 'Done.' It is satisfying to see your progress, and it keeps you from getting overwhelmed by the big picture.

Now, let's tackle the beast that is **procrastination**. It is the archnemesis of productivity, lurking around with distractions like social media notifications or that new series everyone's binge-watching. Beat this beast by **breaking your work into smaller, manageable steps**. Instead of facing a daunting task head-on, chip away at it. Do you need to do a massive report? Start with just the outline, or do some initial research. These baby steps add up, and before you know it, you're halfway there. Plus, giving yourself mini-deadlines for these smaller segments can keep the momentum going without the panic of a last-minute all-nighter.

Keeping a balanced life is not just about getting things done. It's also about making sure you **don't burn out**. To do this, you must **carve out time for relaxation and fun**. It's like giving your car a regular tune-up to keep it running smoothly. **Schedule breaks** like you schedule work. Hit pause for a coffee with friends, a run in the park, or whatever recharges your batteries. Remember, downtime is not wasted time—it's essential maintenance for your brain.

Balancing work, fun, and self-care ensures you're surviving and thriving. Get your priorities straight, arm yourself with some nifty tools, break tasks into bite-sized pieces, and don't forget to recharge your batteries. You'll keep your daily circus act going without dropping the ball. Keep these tricks up your sleeve, and you can keep the show running, wow the crowd, and maybe even surprise yourself.

Conclusion

> *Be here now.*
>
> Ram Dass

No matter what your next big adulting step is, you are embarking on a wild rollercoaster called "Major Life Transition." Let me tell you, it will bring up a cocktail of contradictory emotions. Embrace the madness – none of these feelings are final. They'll be happy and sad, easy and hard, fun and awful, heartbreaking and heart-expanding. You'll spin through the emotional carousel from loneliness and sorrow to exuberance and delight and back again – like a moody boomerang. You can ride it out because it's all normal, and it's all good.

When you hit a big milestone, why not throw a little party or create a quirky ritual to mark the moment? Whether it's an event, a piece of jewelry, or even a tattoo (if that's your thing), marking the occasion with gratitude and hope can make the ride truly special.

Mastering adulthood is not an overnight thing. You'll ace some tasks immediately and mess up others—like when you forget to pay the electricity bill and end up in the dark. But every mistake is just a lesson in disguise.

Continue to build up your life skills, from cooking something better than instant ramen to budgeting your money wisely to handling your workplace dynamics. Each new skill you learn is a step forward in dealing with life's curveballs.

Stay present, folks. When we are in the moment, we stay grounded in the things that make us smile and we're open to the shenanigans happening right before us. Life is coming at you at lightning speed, so take it in and have some fun with all this. Keep the faith and trust the process. It will take you where you need to go at the pace you need to get there, with one heck of an adventure to look back on.

And give yourself some grace, a little pat on the back. Getting a handle on all this adult stuff is no easy task, but you're pulling it off, and that's something to celebrate. Keep pushing, keep learning, and you might discover that adulting can be a blast. So, get out there and tackle your life.

Take this final image with you, which can be helpful in so many situations:

Whatever you must do today, do it with the confidence of a 4-year-old in a Batman cape.

You got this.

You Can Help Others to Adult!

You're on your way to great heights in the real world! You can help guide others on their path to independence with a quick book review.

Simply by sharing your honest opinion of this book and a little about your own experience, you'll make it easy for new readers to find the information they're looking for.

**TAKE A MOMENT TO
SHARE YOUR THOUGHTS!**

Thank you! Your review will have more impact than you might imagine.

Scan the QR code below:

References

Adulting 101: How Not to Move Back Home with Your Parents, Las Hermanas Publishing, Copyright 2022

The Perfect Teenager: Navigate Teen Empowerment, Social Anxieties, Essential Life Lessons in this Modern World Stress-Free, Natalie Stevens, Copyright 2024

How Not to Die Alone: The Surprising Science that Will Help You Find Love, Logan Ury, Piatkus Publishing, Copyright 2021

Be Here Now, Ram Dass, Harmony Publishing, copyright 1978.

What Is a Credit Score? Definition, Factors, and Ways to ... https://www.investopedia.com/terms/c/credit_score.asp

10 Essential Money Tips For Young Adults https://www.forbes.com/sites/enochomololu/2023/09/18/10-essential-money-tips-for-young-adults/

Ultimate Guide: Copper's Guide to Budgeting (for teens) https://www.getcopper.com/guide/budgeting

Investing for Teens: What They Should Know https://www.investopedia.com/investing-for-teens-7111843

21 Side Hustles for Teens to Make Extra Cash in 2024 https://millennialmoney.com/side-hustles-for-teens/

How to Negotiate Your Starting Salary https://hbr.org/2022/07/how-to-negotiate-your-starting-salary

5 Tips for How to File Taxes for the First Time - TurboTax - Intuit https://turbotax.intuit.com/tax-tips/general/tips-for-how-to-file-taxes-for-the-first-time/L6nNi6uJn

How to Build or Rebuild Your Credit Using a Secured Credit Card | HuffPost Life. https://www.huffpost.com/entry/how-to-build-or-rebuild-y_b_5335355

How to Help Teens Build Emotional Intelligence https://www.newportacademy.com/resources/empowering-teens/teen-emotional-intelligence/

Teen Stress: 10 Stress-Management Skills for Teenagers https://www.newportacademy.com/resources/mental-health/teen-stress-relief/

5 Strategies for Teaching Empathy to Teens https://www.connectionsacademy.com/support/resources/article/teaching-empathy-to-teens/

Amazing Quotes. https://amazing-quotes.in/motivational/3690/

What Teens Need to Know About Boundaries https://www.verywellfamily.com/boundaries-what-every-teen-needs-to-know-5119428

Teenagers and Communication - Better Health Channel https://www.betterhealth.vic. gov.au/health/healthyliving/teenagers-and-communication

The Importance of Social Media Etiquette: An Insight for ... https://www.linkedin.com/ pulse/importance-social-media-etiquette-insight-individuals-mani-maran

11 Public Speaking Tips for Youth (and Adults!) - Venture Lab https://venturelab.org/ public-speaking-tips/

25 skills every cook should know https://www.bbcgoodfood.com/howto/guide/25-skills-every-cook-should-know

10 Easy Ways to Grocery Shop on a Budget https://www.ramseysolutions.com/budget ing/10-easy-ways-to-grocery-shop-on-a-budget

Tips for Teens- Laundry How To https://successfulhomemakers.com/tips-for-teens-laundry-how-to/

8 Time Management Tips for Students - Harvard Summer School https://summer. harvard.edu/blog/8-time-management-tips-for-students/

5 Financial Scams to Watch Out For in 2023 https://www.cnbc.com/select/financial-scams-how-to-avoid/

How Social Media Affects Your Teen's Mental Health https://www.yalemedicine.org/ news/social-media-teen-mental-health-a-parents-guide

Cyberbullying: What is it and how to stop it - UNICEF https://www.unicef.org/end-violence/how-to-stop-cyberbullying

15 Ways to Find Your Passion in Life | Indeed.com https://www.indeed.com/career-advice/finding-a-job/how-to-find-your-passion

The Future of Jobs Report 2023 | World Economic Forum https://www.weforum.org/ publications/the-future-of-jobs-report-2023/digest/

Trade School vs College: What's the Difference and Which Is ... https://intercoast.edu/ articles/trade-school-vs-college-whats-the-difference-and-which-is-best-for-you/

21 Helpful Internship Tips for Success (With Importance) https://www.indeed.com/ career-advice/starting-new-job/internship-tips

Youth in the Justice System: An Overview https://jlc.org/youth-justice-system-over view

Minors and Contract Law: Everything You Need to Know https://www.upcounsel.com/ minors-and-contract-law

Children's Online Privacy Protection Rule ("COPPA") https://www.ftc.gov/legal-library/browse/rules/childrens-online-privacy-protection-rule-coppa

www.ingramcontent.com/pod-product-compliance
Lightning Source LLC
Chambersburg PA
CBHW060241030426
42335CB00014B/1568